MEDIA STUDIES

AN INTRODUCTION TO JOURNALISM

MICHAEL BROMLEY

Hodder & Stoughton
A MEMBER OF THE HODDER HEADLINE GROUP

British Library Cataloguing in Publication Data

Bromley, Michael
  Media Studies: Introduction to Journalism
  I. Title
  070.4

ISBN 0-340-64401-X

First published 1994 as *Teach Yourself Journalism*
Re-published 1995 as *Media Studies: An Introduction to Journalism*
Impression number   10 9 8 7 6 5 4 3 2 1
Year   1999 1998 1997 1996 1995

Copyright © 1994, 1995 Michael Bromley

All rights reserved. No part of this publication may be reproduced or
transmitted in any form or by any means, electronic or mechanical,
including photocopy, recording, or any information storage and
retrieval system, without permission in writing from the publisher
or under licence from the Copyright Licensing Agency Limited.
Further details of such licences (for reprographic reproduction)
may be obtained from the Copyright Licensing Agency Limited,
of 90 Tottenham Court Road, London W1P 9HE.

Typeset by Rowland Phototypesetting Ltd, Bury St Edmunds, Suffolk.
Printed in Great Britain for Hodder & Stoughton Educational,
a division of Hodder Headline Plc, 338 Euston Road, London NW1 3BH
by Cox & Wyman Ltd, Reading, Berks.

CONTENTS

Preface	v
Acknowledgements	vi
1 What is journalism?	1
The news room	3
Learning about journalism	8
2 Journalism	10
'Serious' and tabloid journalism	10
Standards of journalism	12
Recruitment into journalism	13
A 'nose' for news?	14
Status and salary	15
Journalistic relationships and social mobility	16
Specialist journalism	18
3 Journalists	20
NCTJ	21
Moving on	23
The broad areas of journalism	23
What does a 'journalist' do?	24
The established patterns of progression	25
4 Skills	28
Personal qualities	29
Skills	31
Knowledge	34
Journalism – an exclusive club	37
5 Multi-skilling	41
Newspapers	42
Broadcasting	44
The future	48

6	The media	53
	National and provincial press	53
	Television and radio	59
	Magazines	60
	Books	62
	A media explosion?	63
7	The media 'revolution'	64
	Provincial press	71
8	The media 'revolution': 2	75
	Television	75
	Radio	79
	Magazines	80
	Books	82
9	News	85
	What is news?	88
10	'Good' news versus 'bad' news	94
11	Objectivity	101
	Photography	107
12	Ethics	110
13	Getting started	138
	Training and courses	142
	Useful sources of information	143
	Training opportunities	144
14	'Why I want to be a journalist'	149
	Taking off	152
15	Resources	164
	What is journalism?	164
	Journalism	164
	Journalists	165
	Skills	165
	Multi-skilling	165
	English	166
	The media	166
	Media 'revolution'	167
	Objectivity	167
	Ethics	167
	Getting started	168
	Starting salaries	168
Index		**169**

PREFACE

Few working journalists think a great deal about how they do their job. Proficiency in journalism is still largely acquired through a process more akin to osmosis than analysis.

Being relieved of the pressure of meeting deadlines undoubtedly provides the best opportunity to reflect on how journalists work. Being subjected at the same time to requests for explanations about how journalists do their job makes such reflection imperative. In more than 20 years working as a journalist I thought a great deal less about journalism than I have in four years' teaching.

This is not always seen as a good thing. The majority opinion among practising journalists in the United Kingdom probably remains that people in universities and colleges actually think too much about journalism. The situation is changing, however. Journalism is slowly becoming a graduate occupation. Audiences are more critically aware. Media owners are more commercially driven. At the same time, journalism as a subject has been appearing more frequently in further and higher education courses. This is largely as a result of student demand. In each instance, there is a demand for increased understanding of journalism. This book is a product of these circumstances.

Students at Luton College of Higher Education (now the University of Luton) and City University pointed out the absence of a book which gathered together the material required to introduce journalism as a subject, rather than one which either attempted to instruct them how to be journalists, or applied the theories and methods of the academic disciplines of media and communications studies without engaging with journalism practically. Among colleagues (both journalists and teachers) the changing nature and expectations of readers, listeners and viewers, the developments in the media businesses, the close inter-relationships between the two and the impact they are having on journalism are a prime concern.

This means that this book is not light reading. Journalism does have a role in entertaining its audiences. The extent to which it is now regarded as a part of show business, or as a small component of the leisure industry, however, is itself seen by many as an extremely serious matter. For the most part, I hope that I have left the readers to make up their own minds whether journalism is a product no different from a bar of chocolate, or of no more social importance than a comedy act — or if it is essentially a public service without which the liberal democratic process would function far less effectively.

As I have already made obvious, many people contributed (even if unknowingly) to this book. In particular Bruce Hanlin and Annabel Hobley read the text and made many helpful suggestions and comments, and Adrian Page helped me to work out my approach to the subject.

Responsibility for the shortcomings of what appears here remains mine alone, of course.

Michael Bromley
City University, January 1995

Acknowledgements

For permission to include copyright material in this book the author and publishers are grateful to: Westminster Press (Figure 5.1); the National Union of Journalists (Table 4.1, which first appeared in *The Journalist*, and Figures 12.1, 12.3 and 12.4); ITN (Figure 5.2); the Campaign for Press and Broadcasting Freedom (Figure 12.6); the BBC (Figure 7.1); the Press Standards Board of Finance (Figure 12.2), and the Periodical Publishers' Association (Figure 12.5).

1

WHAT IS JOURNALISM?

> '"Now we've gotter write news," said William.
> "But there isn't any news," objected Henry.
> "Newspapers don't only say news," contributed
> Ginger with an air of deep wisdom, "they
> sort of say what they sort of think of
> things. They sort of write about things they
> don't like, an' about people doing things
> they don't like." William brightened. "We
> could easy do that," he said.'
>
> Richmal Crompton
> *William in Trouble* (1962)

Every day most of us watch, listen to, or read something called 'journalism'. What is it? Who are the journalists? Where do they get their material? How do they decide what goes into the paper or broadcast? Why do journalists always seem to get things wrong? When does something become news? There aren't many straightforward answers to these questions.

There are about 35,000 practising journalists in the United Kingdom, it is thought. Research begun in 1994 at the London College of Printing was the first to try to establish both the precise numbers and the actual experiences of journalists. Of these, as many as 75 per cent (about 26,000) were members of the main trade union, the National Union of Journalists (NUJ).

Because journalism in the United Kingdom has been primarily learned on the job, journalism training has emphasised the value of experience. The beginner needed to show from the outset an 'aptitude' to learn from experience, and to acquire journalistic know-how. All journalists, therefore, were supposed to have an instinctive 'news sense'. Journalists, it was often said, were born and not made. This gave rise to a tendency to see certain 'types' as being more likely to develop into successful journalists.

Journalism then was the product of instinct and experience. Writing a news story (or a feature article, or a sports report, or a press release) was not like removing a gall-bladder. It was not a procedure, defined and written up in textbooks. There were no formulas for one well-written article leading to another. An old journalism adage stated that any journalist was only as successful as the last article they had written. At a time when video and audio cassette recorders, photocopiers and scanners have led to many media products being kept and re-used, it is easy to overlook the essentially specific and ephemeral nature of journalism. 'Literature,' the British journalist Cyril Connolly wrote, 'is the art of writing something that will be read twice; journalism what will be grasped at once.' Journalism traded on its immediacy and accessibility.

Journalism was also part of a major industry worth about £35 billion a year. Its output in one form or another reached at least three-quarters of the British population. In the late 1980s and early 1990s more than £3 billion was invested in the media in the United Kingdom. The £1.5 billion invested in BSkyB, the satellite television broadcaster, was the second largest single private investment ever in British industry. The major force in journalism since the 1980s has been its confrontation with the market. Where once the journalist's 'nose for news' was trusted to detect the mood of the public, increasingly sophisticated market research has been used to provide more concrete objective evidence of popular taste. Much of this evidence has shown that the media compete among themselves for the attention, and the £s, of the public. Journalism has become one product among many in an extended leisure market.

The news room

Until very recently news rooms in newspapers, radio, television, or magazines were much the same. A journalist would feel at home in almost any one they found themselves in. The structure, the titles and the sheer size might have differed from medium to medium, and from paper to paper, or station to station (see Figure 1.1). The clutter, the atmosphere, the noise, much of the jargon and the *ambience* didn't. This was largely because the principles on which they were founded were the same. Every news room contained three broad categories of journalists (although some straddled more than one category) – the news gatherers (reporters, photographers), news processors (sub-editors) and news managers (section editors in news, pictures, and sub-editing).

Much the same organisation was replicated in other editorial departments (if indeed they were separate entities); for example, in sport and in features. Over all this there was a higher executive level headed by the editor, and probably including a deputy, and a number of assistants. The structural separation between reporters, sub-editors, managers and higher executives tended to lead to divisiveness, although it was often called 'creative tension'. This meant that hierarchies were steep and the working rules of the news room rigid to try to keep all the parts operating together.

The system evolved with the development of the modern mass circulation press, and later radio and television, starting at the end of the last century. It gave rise to some of the most enduring images of journalism presented in literature and films such as *Scoop*, *The Front Page* and *Brighton Rock* – the powerful, ambitious editor; the cantankerous, conniving news editor; the seedy, shifty reporter; and the organisational chaos of journalism generally. It also lent itself to another set of views on journalism; that of a crusading, incorruptible profession, embodied in the restless investigative reporter, backed by a fearless editor, exposing hypocrisy and corruption.

While layers of executives and managers demanded loyalty and obedience – the editor's word was always final – in practice it was difficult to exercise complete authority over such diverse and sometimes large groups of people who, of necessity, worked a lot of the time on their own initiative. Journalists also appeared to be slightly anarchistic, self-willed and essentially uncontrollable. On a day-to-day basis what primarily tied the potentially disparate parts of the news room together

JOURNALISM

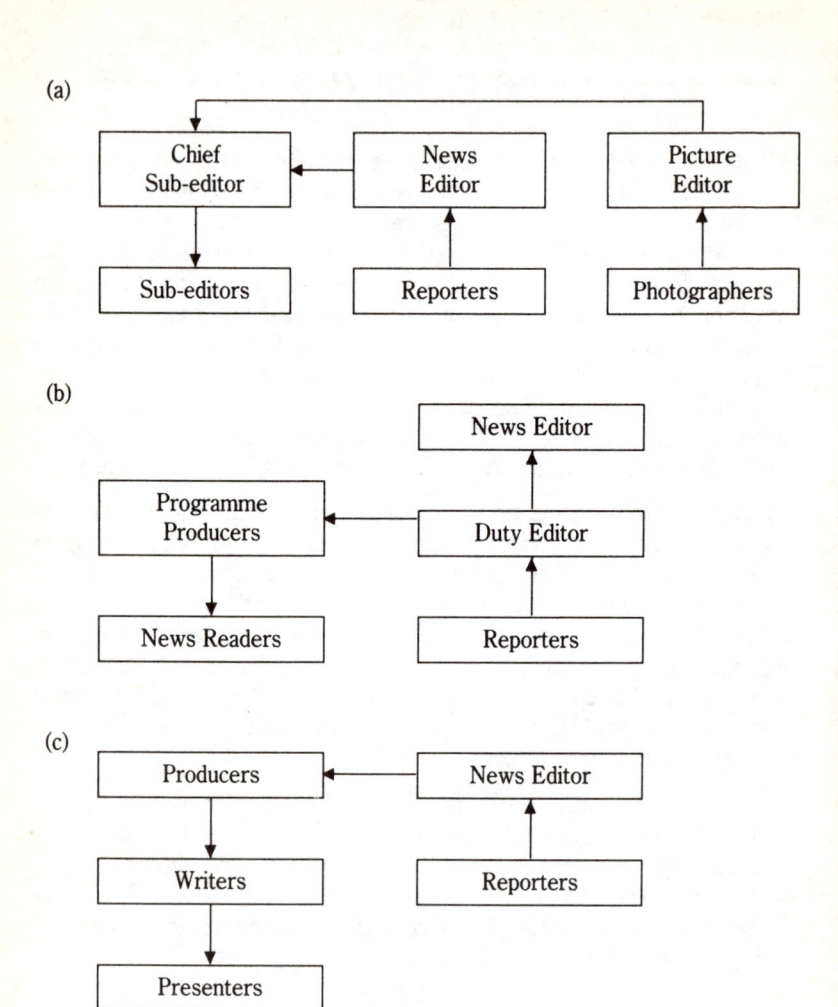

Figure 1.1: Simplified diagrams of typical news room structures and copy flow [→] of (a) a newspaper; (b) a local radio station; (c) television

were shared 'professional' values, and the process of getting the paper, the magazine, or the bulletin out.

The path followed by the material that was eventually to make up the paper, the magazine or the bulletin was fundamentally linear – from news gatherers *via* news managers to news processors and then back through the managers to executives for final approval. At each point of transfer in the chain, there was commonly a separate dialogue between only the people immediately involved. The process, therefore, was made up essentially of a series of individual transactions. Although journalists liked to consider the news desk to be the hub of the news room, around which all activities revolved, it was more accurately described as a link in an extended chain.

A written and completed news article would go through this kind of 'copy flow' in a newspaper news room:

> reporter to news editor
> news editor to chief sub-editor
> chief sub-editor to page sub-editor
> page sub-editor to text sub-editor

The obvious advantage of the system was that at several critical points the story was checked by someone other than the author, and with different priorities: was the article accurate? was it fair? written in the correct style? newsworthy? the right length? in good taste? the sort of thing this newspaper wanted to print?

Scripts in broadcasting, and particularly local radio, might follow neither so long nor so linear a route. Nevertheless, checking and double-checking remained central to the process, and there was a clear line of responsibility stretching from reporter *via* producer and bulletin editor to news editor and, eventually, programme controller.

A great deal of journalism, therefore, was effectively hidden and conducted in offices. The reporter (or at a more rarefied level, the editor) who met the public was the exception. When Westminster Press, a major provincial press owner, researched the practices of one of its newspaper centres in 1994, it could identify only 38 per cent of the journalists' time dedicated to gathering material. Such findings made it certain that traditional news room practices would be challenged and very likely changed.

This has already happened in some areas of broadcasting. Independent local radio stations have begun operating with only one or two journalists (sometimes part-timers) who undertake all the news room work. Some provincial newspapers have suggested that news gatherers should also process work. National newspapers have started tentatively along a similar route. At the same time, the disciplines of business and marketing were invading the news room. Journalists, who previously had relied on their own skills and experience to determine the newsworthiness of information, began to be guided by market research which reported what interested audiences. In the 1990s journalism was changing.

In order to make sense of those changes it was necessary to understand existing practices. Like any other job, journalism had both its mysteries and its own peculiar language. Much of both were not only arcane but also archaic. For 80 years of the twentieth century journalism had been dominated by a production process founded in the techniques of the 1880s. The development of broadcasting began to have an impact only in the 1960s, and the real changes resulting from that became irreversible in the 1980s.

In journalism a great deal of the old persisted alongside the new. By the 1990s journalism was a mixture of tradition, lodged in the relatively ancient art of printing, and of an emerging future of digitalised global communications. Journalists' basic tools remained ink and paper, even where they also relied on satellite links, portable computers and electronic imaging. In many offices the standard glossary of printing terms on the journalist's desk sat next to a computer manual. The jargon, which journalists were constantly urged to avoid in their writing, was still a feature of life in the news room.

Dozens of terms disappeared from current usage – among them, oddities such as *chase* (the metal frame in which type was assembled before printing) and *stick* (either the tray in which type was put together by hand, or about two-and-a-half inches of type). In many cases they were replaced by new terms, and, of course, the basic language of journalism – that of *embargoes*, *inside-backs* and *nibs* – continued unabashed. What follows is a basic collection to act as a guide:

Glossary

Actuality   recording of actual event, or someone speaking
Ad   abbreviation for advertisement
Audio   sound material

WHAT IS JOURNALISM?

Back-bench — senior editorial executives of a newspaper
Broadsheet — newspaper page size (approx. 23ins by 16ins), used to describe the **quality press**
Bulletin — news programme (UK); news item (USA)
Byline — reporter's name appearing with a **story**
Classified — small **ads**
Compositor — the man (always) who composed or made up the metal **type**
Copy — the written material produced by newspaper journalists; sometimes used by broadcast journalists
Copy flow — the route along which **copy** moves
Correspondent — (i) journalist covering a specific place or area (as in, Paris Correspondent, or village correspondent); (ii) specialist journalist (Political Correspondent; Show Business Correspondent)
Deadline — the time at which **copy** is required
Display — large **ads**
Dub — copy recording from one tape to another
Editing — amending and checking **copy** and **tape**; also, the work of an **editor**
Editor — most senior editorial executive; in newspapers legally responsible for all contents of the paper
Embargo — prohibition on publishing before a specified time; **press releases** are often distributed in advance and embargoed
Feature — an article appearing in a newspaper that is not news
Feature writer — journalist who writes **features**, as opposed to news (written by **reporters**)
Freelance — journalist not on the editorial staff; self-employed
Headline — the heading to **text**
Inside back — the next to last page (the one inside the back page)
Keystroking — word processing (or any form of typing)
Layout — the design of a newspaper page
Middle-market — the press standing between the **quality** and the **tabloid** newspapers, e.g. *Daily Mail*
Newsprint — the paper on which newspapers are printed

Nib	paragraphs of news usually in a column (from 'News in brief')
Package	report made up of journalist's contribution and **actuality**
Pagination	number of pages
Pictures	photographs
Producer	person in broadcasting responsible for putting the **bulletin** on air
Quality	up-market, **broadsheet** newspapers
Reporter	journalist principally concerned with gathering news
Script	broadcast journalist's **copy**
Story	article, or potential article
Sub-editor	journalist who checks, corrects and prepares **copy** for printing
Tabloid	page size (half that of **broadsheet**), used to describe the down-market press
Text	the main printed material in a newspaper, as distinct from headlines, graphics, photographs, etc.
Web offset	printing process

Learning about journalism

This is not a journalism manual. It is not possible to learn how to be a journalist by reading about journalism. The vast majority of people without prior experience who want to practise journalism in one form or another, however, have very little idea what journalism is. This book represents an attempt to rectify this. It is *about* journalism – what journalism is, where it is practised, by whom, how and why. This is an essential starting-point. Few editors, journalism course directors and interviewing panels expect aspiring journalists to have any real practical journalism experience. The tradition in Britain rests heavily on learning while actually doing the job. All the same, potential employers are inevitably impressed by (and may even expect) an awareness of journalism as it is practised. This is one way of distinguishing between the hundreds, or even thousands, of applicants attracted to every available post in journalism.

Journalism may not be a self-regulating profession in the same sense as medicine and the law are, but journalists are nevertheless 'professional' in many ways. Comparative practices, the history of journalism, the politics of the press, media economics, ethics, and the impact of change are actively debated. It has to be admitted that the more abstract concerns have been less in evidence in the past decade or so. Sheer economic pressures have focused journalists' attentions onto more prosaic matters, to the extent that many have not looked beyond the struggle to keep their audiences satisfied, their publications in business and their programmes on air, or even just their own jobs. Yet this attitude has itself begun to emerge as a central element in the broader and more vigorous debate over general standards in journalism. The fact that journalists have ceased to be as active in analysing their precise role in the media and in society as a whole has contributed to a climate of crude commercialism, especially in the 'popular' press, which has promoted escalating sensationalism for profit.

Because the media have traditionally been claimed and been accorded a part in the public debate essential for parliamentary democracy, these trends have been criticised as harmful to the political process. There is talk now of a 'lost generation' of journalists which has abandoned its 'professionalism', and of the need to restore a 'professional' perspective to journalism. The *British Journalism Review* argued in 1989,

> 'Perhaps the greatest weakness of British journalism, when we compare it with the journalism of many other European countries, as well as with some of the best American journalism, has been its lack of a reflective and analytical culture.'

The process of review may be as uncomfortable as it is reassuring. The media are undergoing enormous change – perhaps greater than for a century or more. Audiences and their expectations have changed most of all. If journalists really do begin to think 'professionally' again about what they do, they will undoubtedly find that many of the cosy assumptions of the past are no longer valid. Restoring 'professional' debate in journalism, therefore, is not simply about returning untroubled to a previous golden age. Young people entering journalism today have possibly unprecedented opportunities to help to determine the shape of journalism and the media for both the present and the future. To be able to do so, they need to be informed; to be critically aware of journalism, its practices and its practitioners. That remains the most valid point of departure for any aspiring journalist.

2

JOURNALISM

> '... broken-down sharpers, *ci-devant* markers
> at gambling houses and the very worst
> description of uneducated blackguards.'

While most people would not use precisely the same words as E. Bulwer-Lytton did 160 years ago, journalists have often seemed to be held in as low esteem in the late twentieth century. In an opinion poll in 1993 in which professionals were ranked according to how truthful people thought they were, journalists came far below doctors, teachers and lawyers, and even politicians. Although the situation is not new – efforts were made in Bulwer-Lytton's time to rectify the poor image of journalists – the development of the tabloid press since 1970 is seen as having made a significant contribution to the lowering of the prestige of journalism. One way of handling this has been to divide journalism into the 'serious' and the 'popular'.

'Serious' and tabloid journalism

The distinction between 'serious' and tabloid journalism has been unclear in Britain, whereas in the United States of America a strict division has been established. Tabloid journalism has been disowned by journalism at large. Eddie Clontz, editor of the tabloid *Weekly World News*, has admitted, 'We're the French Foreign Legion of journalism.' Contemporary American tabloid journalism was largely based on the Fleet Street model of the 1970s and 1980s. Initially, most of the journalists on American tabloids were British with what one of them, Phil

Bunton, editorial director of Globe Communications, publisher of the *National Examiner*, *Globe* and *Sun*, called a 'talent to sensationalise'. The *Star*, established by Rupert Murdoch, was modelled on his London papers *The Sun* and *News of the World*. Yet, while the American tabloids are not legally classified as newspapers (they are regarded as magazines), the Fleet Street titles are mainstream, and they have been seen as having exercised an overriding influence on setting the news agenda for all the media. In February 1994, the *Guardian* asked, 'Are we witnessing the tabloiding of Britain?'

Conventional definitions of journalism emphasise the importance of news, and stress the rational communication of political, economic and social ideas and information. The news media are supposed to stimulate and reflect the citizen's concern with government; to be an integral part of the democratic process. The notion of the press as the Fourth Estate, which emerged at the beginning of the nineteenth century, saw newspapers as providing an extra-parliamentary platform, and performing the function of a watchdog on the State. Journalism was to act as a custodian of the public interest; its mission was to tell the truth, fearlessly and freely. The observation of C. P. Scott, editor and later proprietor of the *(Manchester) Guardian*, that 'Comment is free but facts are sacred' has come to summarise this approach. Scott wrote about the press

> 'Its primary office is the gathering of news. At the peril of its soul it must see that the supply is not tainted. Neither in what it gives, nor in what it does not give, nor in the manner of presentation, must the unclouded face of truth suffer wrong.'
> *Manchester Guardian* (6 May 1926)

It has been difficult, however, to reconcile this kind of dedication to 'truth' with headlines such as FREDDIE STAR ATE MY HAMSTER and WORLD WAR II BOMBER FOUND ON MOON. Is this kind of journalism simply a parody? Nearly half the people surveyed in America in 1984 did not believe that the tabloids were accurate. However, less than a quarter who took part in another poll trusted regular newspapers either. The tabloid press has been criticised for diverting from what one journalist has called 'that fundamental respect for truth'.

Of course, there has been little really new in tabloid journalism as such: it has probably existed in some form for 300 years. Contemporary tabloids claim they are following in the traditions of many of the founding figures of modern journalism, such as the Americans William Randolph

Hearst and Joseph Pulitzer, or in Britain Alfred Harmsworth (Lord Northcliffe), the founder of the *Daily Mail* and *Daily Mirror* who was determined that his papers should be respectable. (He also owned the *Times*.) There have been times when it has seemed possible to serve the best intentions of both 'serious' and 'tabloid' journalism to produce informative, interesting, entertaining and accessible material on a range of issues, for example, in the *Daily Mirror* of the 1960s and the *Sunday Times* Insight investigative journalism of the 1970s.

Standards of journalism

There was nothing new either in complaints about the standards of journalism. The emergence of modern 'popular' journalism at the end of the nineteenth century was felt by many to be an expression of low, 'commonplace' taste. The Conservative Prime Minister Lord Salisbury sniffily dismissed the *Daily Mail* (founded in 1896) as 'Written by office boys for office boys'. Proponents of 'serious' journalism tried to maintain that their approach was different: the editor of the *Observer* J. L. Garvin insisted, 'I mean to give the public what they *don't* want'. Nevertheless, establishing the difference was not always easy, and in a celebrated aphorism Oscar Wilde observed

> 'There is much to be said in favour of modern journalism. By giving us the opinions of the uneducated, it keeps us in touch with the ignorance of the community.'
> *The Critic as Artist*, Part 2

Yet there has been perhaps more serious concern over the standards of journalism in the 1980s and 1990s than at any previous time. There has been a mounting criticism of the tastes and practices of journalism – of invasions of privacy; of inaccuracies and distortions; of concentration on the trivial and titillating. Nor has this debate been conducted exclusively among the 'chattering classes': the ways in which journalists do their jobs have become the subject of television drama and comedy shows, such as Drop the Dead Donkey and Spitting Image. Journalists a century ago were generally regarded admiringly (if sometimes grudgingly) as slightly bohemian, 'lively, brash men and women'. By the 1990s they were often seen as highly regulated and well-paid producers of 'porno-populism'. Asked to list the characteristics they automatically associated most with journalists, respondents to a survey in 1993 replied 'aggressive', followed by 'not my kind of person'.

—— Recruitment into journalism ——

On the other hand, there has been no shortage of recruits into journalism. Most vacancies for traineeships have been filled without being advertised. Those which are, such as two with the *Sunday Times* for graduates, have attracted thousands of applications. Higher education courses at both first degree and postgraduate level have also been heavily oversubscribed. To some extent the attraction of journalism has been cyclical. Periodically cases such as the investigation of the Watergate affair in the 1970s by the *Washington Post* journalists Carl Bernstein and Bob Woodward have raised the profile of journalism and led to an upsurge in interest. In the 1980s work in the media took on a higher profile and a new glamour. There was a growth in the number of jobs in magazine and radio journalism, and a raising of salaries and status for many established journalists in the national media. What may have had most impact, however, was a steady decline in the number of options for employment for the 'typical' journalism recruit: the school-leaver with an aptitude for English, or the arts graduate.

Graduate recruitment into journalism expanded rapidly from the later 1960s. Even in the provincial press, which traditionally looked for its journalists in local schools and colleges, about 50 per cent of recruits were graduates by 1990. Magazines were taking on four times as many graduates as non-graduates. National newspapers, including the *Sunday Times*, *Daily Express*, and *Daily Mirror*, instituted graduate training schemes where once they relied chiefly on recruiting trained journalists from the provincial press. Radio and television, led by the BBC, strongly favoured graduate recruitment, and the approach of public relations was similar. This trend towards graduate recruitment could be seen as indicating the *type* of person to whom journalism might have appealed, and who was likely to be seen by employers as a potential journalist.

A 'nose' for news?

Thirty years ago it was common to hear that journalists were 'born and not made': to be successful journalists needed what was rather mysteriously called 'a nose for news'. A great deal of academic media analysis and a smaller amount of self-criticism have done much to dispel such over-simplifications: journalists learn through various means how to produce news. All the same, the old ideas have proved to be tenacious. In a 1993 edition of a guide to newspaper reporting approved by the National Council for the Training of Journalists (NCTJ) the skills learned in training were derided as 'mechanics'. The authors wrote, '. . . whether you become a good reporter or not depends on whether you have this eye [an interesting variant on the "nose" theme] for news'. Most journalism manuals at least mention, and some stress, this intuitive approach. Why has the mystique persisted?

Since the 1970s management and work practices in all the media have undergone fundamental change. This has had quite dramatic effects on journalism. On the one hand, the introduction of computer technology has led to journalists gaining more control over their work by increasingly inputting directly into the production process. On the other hand, however, the numbers of journalists employed by individual newspapers, magazines, or radio or television stations have fallen. Many have begun working on short-term contracts or on a freelance basis, rather than as full-time salaried members of staff. As a general practice managements have replaced flexible industrial relations, and union by union negotiations with centralised human resource management favouring standardised personal contracts.

Simultaneously journalists, like professionals in medicine, teaching, the law and elsewhere, have had their traditional authority to determine largely for themselves the ways in which they carry out their duties challenged, not just by employers but also by their customers: people have become less inclined to accept that the expert knows best. Because journalism is not formally a profession, and is neither recognised nor regulated as such, it has been particularly vulnerable to these changes.

Status and salary

A small minority of journalists, chiefly in television, radio and national newspapers, have become *more* powerful and increasingly 'professional'. They have attained celebrity status, and have exercised considerable influence. As Professor Jeremy Tunstall has said, they can 'look politicians . . . in the eye'. As a reflection of their status, they have earned large sums of money, often from several sources.

Anne Robinson reputedly earned at least £200,000 a year for writing a column in *Today* newspaper and a further £200,000 for television and other related work. For the vast majority of anonymous journalists, however, the trend has been in the opposite direction. They have found their jobs de-skilled, with trade union derecognition and computer technology permitting untrained amateurs to earn pin money from casual journalism. A senior reporter with 20 years of experience on a medium sized provincial evening newspaper was earning around £20,000 a year in 1992. Even in the USA, where the status of journalists has normally been much higher, the median income for a journalist with at least 20 years of experience was $40,000 (about £26,000), with both daily newspaper journalists ($35,000 or £23,000) and radio journalists ($20,000 or £13,000) earning less.

Nevertheless, journalists have tried to defend their status and independence. The practice of editors appointing staff largely without reference to corporate human resource management has persisted. The former managing director of a substantial provincial newspaper group noted that his editors had argued successfully that only a journalist can properly judge the qualities and potential of another journalist: they were the only managers in his organisation who appointed staff without consulting the personnel department. A senior television journalist has claimed that management at the BBC has found it difficult to institute changes in practices in news and current affairs because of the resistance of journalists. A manager told researchers that many of the changes the provincial press planned during the 1980s had been frustrated by journalists being 'precious' about their practices.

What has undoubtedly helped in this defence of journalism has been the popular acceptance of the idea of editorial independence; that in the final analysis and whatever the commercial pressures, the media must be free to 'tell the truth' or risk losing their credibility. As the head of the Gannett Center for Media Studies at Columbia University, New York has observed, journalists inhabit 'a somewhat schizophrenic world where pious pronouncements about the pursuit of truth coexist with the obvious need of the press to make profits'. To a considerable extent journalists have been able to argue that their 'nose for news' is a decisive factor in the equation; that they know by instinct the audiences' preferences.

Until relatively recently that position was more or less unassailable: newspapers in particular, but also magazines, did little audience research. Even now that they do much more, journalists may still assert their instinctive approach. When he was appointed editor of the *Times* in 1992, Peter Stothard dismissed the value of market research in determining the quality of his newspaper and insisted instead that the most important factor in attracting and keeping readers was to produce what journalists considered a 'good read'. So the idea of the instinctive journalist may be seen as useful for practising journalists to identify themselves, but it is not necessarily a quick guide to the type of person who might make a career in journalism.

—— Journalistic relationships and —— social mobility

Two additional factors have tended to support the notion of the 'natural' journalist. Firstly there has been a tendency for journalism to run in families. There is no real evidence that this has been more prevalent in journalism than it has in other occupations, such as show business, acting and sport, or even the law and medicine. Moreover, family traditions have been common for centuries in all sections of the printing and publishing industries. Nevertheless journalism dynasties have been established. A notable recent example has been that of the Lawsons. Among his other jobs in journalism, Nigel Lawson, who was later to be Chancellor of the Exchequer, was the features editor, the Lex columnist and a contributor to the *Financial Times*, the editor of the *Spectator* and a contributor to the *Evening Standard*. His son, Dominic, was also the Lex columnist, a *Financial Times* journalist and columnist and in 1990 was appointed the editor of the *Spectator*. His daughter, Nigella, has been the restaurant critic of the *Spectator* and a columnist in the *Evening Standard*.

Another kind of dynastic relationship has been associated with education (and by implication, economic and social background). The upper reaches of journalism have been predominantly occupied by the products of public schools and Oxbridge. Of the 17 men editing national newspapers at the beginning of 1994, at least ten had attended public schools and eight either Oxford or Cambridge universities. The BBC, *Financial Times* and *Economist* in particular have had reputations for preferring Oxbridge graduates almost exclusively. When Roger Bolton, later a highly regarded television producer, joined the BBC as a general trainee from Liverpool University in 1967, he was the only (token) non-Oxbridge recruit: 'I crept in . . . ,' he said. In 1994 there were four Old Etonians (OEs), including the editor, Charles Moore, among the journalists on the *Sunday Telegraph*. Moore said

> 'I'm rather nervous about saying I like being with OEs. But I'm not at all ashamed of appointing them . . . I hate the phrase "the class system", but I do think your background is incredibly important. I mean, if you want to find out about someone the most important thing is to know their family.'
> The *Guardian* (14 February 1994)

Anoja Dias, who was born into a lower middle-class family, re-invented herself in 1991 as a public school and Oxford-educated daughter of a diplomat to embark on a career in journalism. She was hired by the BBC, *Sunday Times*, Central Television, *Evening Standard*, Channel 4 News and CNN. She explained later when she had been exposed,

> '. . . everyone else was from famous families, had been to good schools and Oxbridge . . . I am not trying to justify what I did, but the media is (*sic*) not a meritocracy. If you did not go to Oxbridge, you have not got a chance. A good school, family connections, they all help.'
> The *Observer* Life (6 February 1994)

Contrary to this view, journalism has also been an occupation associated with social mobility. Large numbers of journalists in the twentieth century have had their origins in minority and marginalised communities, such as the Jews and the Irish, and especially since the 1950s in the working-class. In the true tradition of journalism, there are plenty of rags-to-riches stories among journalists, typified perhaps by Derek Jameson. He has described himself as 'a slum kid of dubious parentage who had grown up in a home for waifs and strays'. He subsequently edited three national newspapers and became a radio and television personality. Many journalists, and particularly those who entered journalism in the 1940s, 1950s and 1960s, have emphasised its egalitarianism. Mike Randall, a former editor of the *Daily Mail*, has expressed a common view that journalism is 'the only truly classless society'. Nobody, he has claimed

> '. . . cares about where you come from, what your accent or your clothes are like, where you were educated or who your parents were. Prove that you can do the job and you are accepted.'
> *The Funny Side of the Street*
> (London, 1988)

Specialist journalism

Journalism has at the same time expanded its horizons in terms of the subject matter it has addressed. In the nineteenth century the press concentrated on what Harmsworth called 'only a few aspects of life', chiefly in the realms of high politics and (more occasionally) high society. A hallmark of 'popular' journalism was its concern with the private lives of ordinary people epitomised by the 'human interest' story. This has meant that the variety of employment in journalism has expanded, not least in the past 20 years. The amount of specialisation in journalism has also grown enormously. Fifty years ago there were few specialist journalists – principally only in politics, sport and finance and economics. During the 1950s and 1960s there was an expansion of specialist journalism, establishing a trend that probably accelerated in the 1980s. The overwhelming majority of specialist journalists work in magazines covering literally everything from advertising to zoology. People now enter journalism intent on at least starting their careers, if not spending all of them, in areas that until relatively recently were considered to be on the fringes of journalism, if they existed at all – the music press, fashion journalism, television chat show research, consumer investigations, and so on.

Reflecting on these changes in 1992, Christian Tyler of the *Financial Times*, wrote

'... the prevailing ethos 25 years ago was still almost pre-industrial: you were taken on if you were a likely lad (or, much more rarely, lass), you started at the bottom and you learned on the job ... Journalism was a craft, like joinery or weaving, and the first job of the news editor was to knock out of your head any fancy ideas you might have about Writing.'

By comparison in the 1990s, he noted

'Journalism has become more respectable ... It has become fashionable and, in television, glamorously fashionable ... Journalism is today described as a career: it is even described, occasionally, as a profession. These are shocking developments.'
British Journalism Review, 3 (2)

The question all this raised, Tyler argued, was: 'are today's aspiring journalists the same as they ever were?'

3

JOURNALISTS

> 'Many schoolchildren today are
> being given skills that . . . journalists
> and newspaper editors have . . . It is not
> the technology which is the threat but
> that of an emerging generation who know
> how to gather, record, organise and generate data.'
>
> Alan Prosser,
> Editorial Director, Kent Messenger Group

Technically, anyone who has wanted to declare themselves a journalist and get work as a journalist could do so. This open-ness has made it possible for politicians, athletes, entertainers, historians, criminals and many others to have second careers as journalists.

Paradoxically, it became more difficult during the late 1980s for the ordinary individual to break into professional journalism. As the number of jobs in journalism contracted, greater emphasis was placed by employers on formal qualifications in journalism. At the same time, the number of places available on training schemes, especially those run by employers, and particularly those in the magazine sector, declined. The results of these developments were that there were more already qualified and experienced journalists than there were available jobs. Those seeking qualifications were channelled into university and college courses where there was – and still is – considerable expansion, or to private training organisations, which began to proliferate. The largest provincial newspaper groups, the BBC and ITN, and a small number of national newspapers, however, continued to hire unqualified recruits directly from university (or, more rarely, from school).

NCTJ

For 30 years recruitment into journalism was largely regulated, but not controlled, by the NCTJ. The majority of entrants to journalism – up to 750 people each year – came within its aegis, on company training schemes, university courses, or pre-entry college courses that it specifically accredited. The system was fragmented in 1986 when it became possible for companies to run their training schemes outside the NCTJ, and again in 1992 with the introduction of NVQs. (Some of the intricacies of journalism training are explained further in Chapter 13.) In addition, in the 1980s training for magazine journalism (about 200 entrants a year) was formally organised by the Periodicals Training Council (PTC). There has also been a growing trend for journalists entering radio to take specialised courses approved by the National Council for the Training of Broadcast Journalists (NCTBJ). (The BBC and ITN have their own company training schemes.)

Taken together, these developments have probably been mainly responsible for what still remains largely an innovation – the university degree in journalism. These degrees are more and more likely to offer training leading to formal vocational qualifications (under the NVQ scheme); they have been largely practically based, usually combining journalism with more orthodox academic subjects. One consequence of all this activity has been to put the future of the NCTJ in doubt. By 1994 it was predicted that some individual university departments offering courses in journalism would have as many as 800 registered students – more than the annual intake of the NCTJ.

As a result of these changes, the proportion of people embarking on journalism studies or training before finding a job has increased significantly. Moreover, as financial support for students diminishes, the major responsibility for paying for training falls on the trainees themselves. This has produced a criticism that training is a new way of perpetuating, and perhaps extending, some of journalism's elitism: Professor Brian Winston, director of the Centre for Journalism Studies at the University of Wales in Cardiff, has complained,

> 'Our students are enormously talented people, but they are too white, too middle-class, too rich and too south-east.'

Another criticism has been that the dissolution of a single dominant training pathway in favour of a number of different routes into journalism has established a training hierarchy. Some courses are regarded not only as more desirable but as offering better career options. Full-time Postgraduate Diploma and MA courses are increasingly seen as leading to jobs in the national media: for example, students from these courses have secured first jobs (albeit sometimes on temporary or freelance contracts) with organisations such as the *Sunday Times*, ITN, *New Statesman and Society*, the *Guardian*, *Times Higher Education Supplement*, *Elle*, Sky News, the *Times*, *Options* and *The Independent*.

In fact, it may be argued that it has been the attempts to regularise journalism recruitment and training which have been exceptional. Before the 1950s there were many ways of getting a job in journalism, ranging from graduate recruitment to making the tea, and training largely consisted of *ad hoc* learning on the job. The experience of Jack Heald, who retired in 1993 after spending 43 years working for the *Craven Herald* weekly newspaper in West Yorkshire, was typical. 'I began one Monday morning,' he recalled, 'doing a district and with no training whatever. They can set up all the training schools they wish . . . but there is no better training than getting out there and doing the job.'

In any event, technically the NCTJ was responsible for only newspaper journalism. For many journalists, getting in (and getting on in) journalism was a matter of talent, tenacity, luck, or nepotism – or any mixture of these. While it was common for journalists to begin their careers in menial positions on local papers, some went straight into journalism on nationals, in magazines, or in radio and television; the *Times* recruited graduates in the nineteenth century. Many journalists who started in the national media subsequently moved into other occupations. In some cases starting in journalism has been seen as offering advantages for alternative careers – traditionally in politics; for example, Norman Fowler, who has been a Cabinet minister and chairman of the Conservative Party, joined the *Times* on leaving Cambridge in 1961, nine years before becoming an MP; Brian Gould joined the Foreign Office, served in the British embassy in Brussels and taught at Oxford before becoming a reporter and presenter with Thames Television's TV Eye between two terms as a Labour MP.

Moving on

Many individuals have regarded journalism as a training for other types of writing. Jilly Cooper and Ken Follett began in journalism. Journalists such as Michael Parkinson and Sue Lawley have moved into the entertainment business. This has given rise to the criticism that there has been a division (not eradicated by the NCTJ) between 'career journalists', who trained in order to spend most and perhaps all their working lives in journalism, and those who had little interest in training, and for whom journalism (preferably at as high a level as possible) was a temporary occupation and a stepping-off point for a more desirable career elsewhere.

The broad areas of journalism

For most people the word 'journalist' has most likely meant a television reporter talking to camera; a newspaper correspondent reporting from a war zone; a magazine writer reviewing a rock concert; or a radio news presenter interviewing a studio guest. As varied as these examples are, they represent only a small sample of the wide range of work journalists have done. There have been seven separate (but connected) broad areas in which journalists have worked:

- newspapers
- news agencies
- magazines
- broadcasting
- press and public relations
- book publishing
- freelancing

What does a 'journalist' do?

The term 'journalist' can be applied to writers, photographers, sub-editors and editors, news presenters and news readers, researchers, copywriters and copy editors, designers and typographers, press and public relations (PR) officers, producers and directors. Each category has been sub-divided and further sub-divided; for example, the writers on a medium sized provincial daily newspaper may commonly have included reporters (sub-divided into general news and specialist reporters, such as those writing on sport); staff correspondents (some covering specific geographical areas, others specialist topics such as politics); feature writers (both general and specialist); and leader writers (responsible for the daily editorial). Many journalists have done little writing as such: sub-editors in both print and broadcasting have been mainly concerned with presentation; with checking, correcting and putting into the appropriate form the work of reporters. Television reporters have had to know something about film direction, and need to be able to liaise with camera crews. Journalists in PR have usually been expected to learn about marketing.

Moving from one kind of job to another, however, has been commonplace. As many journalists trained first as newspaper reporters, almost all of those who worked in other areas had experience of general news writing, and many radio and television journalists had earlier careers in newspapers; for example, Sybil Ruscoe, a presenter on BBC Radio Five Live and a reporter with the BBC Television programme Here and Now, joined the Midland News Association's company training scheme as a school-leaver and later worked for the *Express and Star* in Wolverhampton. Local newspapers in particular (and to a lesser extent, local news agencies) often boasted of the number of successful journalists in the national press and broadcasting who had passed through their hands.

The established patterns of progression

The local and regional newspaper as the principal training ground for journalists has been in decline for much of the 1980s. Moreover, relatively few journalists ever moved from television and radio into newspapers, from magazines to the local press, or from PR to news organisations in either print or broadcasting. To that extent there was always a degree of media specialisation among journalists. Undoubtedly this was determined in part by fame and fortune; that journalists in television and national newspapers in particular commanded higher salaries and greater celebrity status. The ambition of most journalists starting out on a local paper was to work in Fleet Street, for the BBC at Television Centre or Broadcasting House, for ITN, Reuters news agency, or the *Economist*. For the most part, the careers of successful younger journalists have still followed these established patterns.

Jacqui Harper has presented Newsroom South East on BBC Television. She developed an interest in journalism while in the sixth form at school in London. 'I had thought of being a teacher. My parents were keen. But then I saw Marvin Gaye in Baker Street one afternoon and asked if I could interview him . . .' With her interview secured and the help of friends, she launched a school magazine. She also helped produce a student magazine at Sussex University, where she studied English and American literature. On an exchange studentship at the University of California, she worked on a newsletter and the daily paper on campus. When she graduated from Sussex, she got a job at the *Oakland Tribune* newspaper in California. Her duties included general administration, checking copy, interviewing, researching and writing. She also worked for the radio station KDIA at weekends. Returning to Britain, she began working at the BBC in 1988. '. . . there was only one other black person in my section. I felt like a hamster in a cage, quite isolated and on show.'

Piers Morgan was appointed editor of the *News of the World* in 1994 at the age of 28. Although while at school he tried work experience at Lloyd's, 'he always wanted to be a journalist', his father has said. When he left comprehensive school, he completed an NCTJ pre-entry training course at Harlow in Essex, and worked as a trainee journalist with the Surrey and South London newspaper group, which includes the *Sutton Herald*. For about a year he freelanced on national newspapers, in particular *The Sun*, where at 22 he was working as a casual on the night news desk. In 1988 he was offered a staff job, reporting for the pop music column, 'Bizarre'. The following year he became the column's editor. Three years later he was offered a job as an assistant editor at *The Sun* but turned it down. His promotion to the acting editorship of the *News of the World* made him the second youngest national newspaper editor of the twentieth century.

Nicola Davidson became a staff journalist with the *Sunday Times* in 1993. She first approached the paper for work experience after leaving school with three A-levels. She was later one of the first group in the *Sunday Times* training scheme for non-graduates. She spent a year running messages and collecting cuttings from the library, while taking a journalism training course. She also helped to research stories for established journalists. 'There is nothing I would not do for the *Sunday Times*. I have given blood for the paper. I have dived from a stage, given up smoking . . . and worked as a waitress . . .' She was the first recruit into the non-graduate training scheme to secure a job as a journalist when she joined the paper's Style section.

Dermot Murnaghan was the reporter who launched the ITV current affairs programme The Big Story in 1993. He was working on a doctorate in Anglo-Irish relations at Trinity College Dublin when he began freelancing for Canadian television. In 1983 he abandoned the PhD and joined a postgraduate course in newspaper journalism at City University. His first job in journalism was with the *Coventry Evening Telegraph* newspaper. He found established journalists with no further or higher education often suspicious of him. 'You were this graduate, dip. this and that, with a string of letters after your name.' Six months later he joined Channel 4 as a researcher and five years later was a presenter on Channel 4 Business Daily. In 1990 he joined ITN and covered the Gulf War. He presented the news at lunchtime and weekends for ITN.

Anna Pasternak produced a world exclusive story for her newspaper, the *Daily Express*, in 1994 when she interviewed Major James Hewitt on his friendship with the Princess of Wales. In the same month she resigned to work as a freelance journalist. Her first job when she left Oxford University, where she had studied geography, was in the publicity department of the publisher, Quartet. After a year she realised that she had learned a great deal about the media. 'Journalists would ask me to get a good quote, and after a while I thought, "Why don't I do this myself?" When I left university I was very interested in the written word, but I didn't know I wanted to be a journalist.' She left publishing and thought about taking a journalism course, but decided instead to 'get stuck in'. She spent three weeks unpaid with the Peterborough diary column of the *Daily Telegraph*. She then freelanced for six months for the column and the diaries of the *Times* and *Evening Standard*. She wrote a cover story for the *Spectator*, and was approached by the *Daily Express* to write women's features on contract for nine months. She then freelanced again for two years, before returning to the *Daily Express* as a staff feature writer. She specialised in interviewing – she had a regular column, the 'Anna Pasternak Interview' – and she felt that freelancing would be less inhibiting. 'I'm not at all afraid of freelancing because if you get it right you have so much more scope.'

4

SKILLS

Until recently the expectation that almost all entrants to journalism would start out as general reporters on local and regional newspapers set standards for recruits. These stressed the extent to which the skills of journalism were vocational, to be learned on the job in an apprenticeship-type system. Such basic skills were expected to serve journalists for the rest of their careers. As the journalist progressed, these skills were developed rather than new skills being acquired. Trained as a general reporter, a journalist would subsequently be expected to move into specialist journalism simply by adapting the basic skills of making contacts, gathering information, interviewing, writing concisely to deadlines, etc, within a narrower area of interest. Specific knowledge was not normally a prerequisite. A competent, trained journalist was considered adequately equipped to become an arts reporter, an industrial editor, or a lobby correspondent – and, in time, possibly all three. Only when moving away from reporting, either into sub-editing and production, or to broadcasting or public relations, was the journalist believed to require additional skills. Even so, these were minimal and normally regarded as adjuncts: journalists were prized for the bedrock of basic newspaper reporting skills they brought to the sub-editors' table, radio, television and PR.

Yet the actual dedicated skills of journalism were neither extensive nor complex; equivalent, according to the NCTJ newspaper reporting manual, to those of 'an intelligent shorthand typist'. Taken together, this set of requirements made journalism particularly attractive as an occupation in which recruits could immediately get out into the 'real world' without having to spend years studying and sitting qualifying examinations, as engineers, accountants, solicitors and many others did. For their part employers (and specifically editors), who did not traditionally place an undue emphasis on educational achievement, looked instead for the personal qualities which it was felt equipped recruits to enter journalism successfully.

Personal qualities

There has been a remarkable consensus about the personal qualities required by journalists. The NCTJ handbook *Training in Journalism*, first published in 1952, said,

> 'Editors look for young people with energy, common sense, the ability to get on with people easily and to work quickly and accurately.'

A National Union of Journalists' (NUJ) pamphlet, produced 40 years later, noted

> 'Journalists need the ability to meet, talk with, and gain the confidence of all sorts of people . . . You need an enquiring mind and an appetite for information . . . You need to be painstakingly accurate.'
>
> *Careers in Journalism* (NUJ, 1993)

The basis for such assertions was that a key area of journalism lay in gathering information and opinion from other people; that journalists primarily asked questions and *listened*. A whole range of further personal qualities was suggested by this approach: confidence without brashness; the ability to see the larger picture without discounting attention to detail; being deductive but not dogmatic. In the words of the NUJ pamphlet cited above,

> 'You should be persistent but not rude; sympathetic but not gullible; sceptical but not cynical . . . You should understand the views of others, and represent them fairly, whether or not you agree with them.'

The intellectual flexibility explicit in this has been matched by the degree of adaptability expected in journalists' attitudes to their working routine.

Journalism has been, by any standards, potentially full of variety. Any two or three successive issues of a newspaper or magazine, or the news bulletins or current affairs programmes broadcast over two or three days by radio or television, illustrated the large amount of different material journalists handled as a matter of course. General reporters in particular would write, often simultaneously and certainly over a couple of days, on a range of topics. Excluding those obviously written by specialists, the home news stories appearing in one edition of the *Times* on a (rather dull) day in February 1994 included:

- a gas leak and fire at a chemical plant
- two separate murders
- five trials; an appeal; one civil action; four pending court cases, and a row over the sentence imposed in another
- the death of a joy-rider
- a golf club electing its first chairwoman
- dogs attacking children in two separate incidents
- a police operation against crime
- a claim that Britain's motorways are crumbling
- a royal tour
- a decision to paint Blackpool Tower gold
- a workman trapped in a 200ft shaft
- a fatal car crash
- the mugging of an 83-year-old woman
- a protest at a Royal Air Force base
- a possible delay in opening the Channel Tunnel
- Home Office criticism of probation officers
- a show business awards ceremony
- a report on the cost of hangovers

Many of the items were routine: some could not have been predicted, however, and stories may have turned out to be dramatic and catastrophic. As well as variety in the type of stories covered by news reporters, the timing and location of stories also varied.

On this particular day, *Times* London-based home news reporters might have round themselves working in Devon, Bedfordshire, Southampton, Cornwall, Bournemouth, Winchester, Cannes or Australia, as well as in and around London; in court, at press conferences, on a building site, at a dinner in a luxury hotel, going door-to-door, or on the telephone in the office. Clearly much of the work must have been completed during the 'normal' working day; for example, courts normally sit between 10am and 4pm with a break for lunch. Other stories on the list, however, will have required the reporters to be at work probably until midnight, and even to be away from London overnight or longer.

Journalism of this type on most newspapers and in radio and television (though slightly more rarely on magazines) has involved unsocial hours and shift working, and a mixture of office-based work and travel (usually to places no more glamorous than Wakefield, Portsmouth and Heathrow Airport). Journalism has been task-oriented, and journalists have been expected to stay with a story to the end. Such mobility and flexibility suggest that, although they have been subject to supervision and direction, like many professionals, journalists have taken a large amount of responsibility for their own work. Initiative and creativity (often expressed as 'having ideas' and following them through) have been highly sought after.

Skills

The skills of journalism have been clustered around a version of the three Rs – research, reproduction and writing.

Research

As has already been noted, journalists' research has been conducted primarily among people – identifying those who can provide information and comment, and contacting and interviewing them. While establishing interpersonal relationships may often be a matter more of personality than skill, nevertheless it has been seen as a central part of journalism to develop techniques in this area. Journalism courses have included training in interviewing and one of the five sections of the NCTJ Proficiency Test has been dedicated to interviewing.

Journalists have not relied exclusively on people for their sources, however: a key question any potential journalist has traditionally been asked by an employer is, *How much do you read?* Surveys have shown that journalists rely heavily on the work of other journalists in newspapers and magazines and on radio and television as sources. Journalism has also involved sifting through, reading, analysing and reporting on written material ranging from two-paragraph press releases to multi-volume official reports. In addition, journalists have always used standard (usually printed) reference material, and most have acquired the skills needed to interpret company records, balance sheets and government papers. Few journalists would claim to be either speed readers or academic researchers, but they have been expected to develop skills to manage the vast amounts of information (the bulk of it still in written form) that has come their way. That task has become increasingly complex (and, it may be argued, more important) as communications have grown in sophistication (see below).

Reproduction

Journalists have been expected not simply to gather material but to disseminate it in a form accessible and relevant to their audiences. There is supposed to have been a time when all the equipment a journalist needed was a notebook and a pencil. Some journalists have claimed to have worked effectively with no more, and perhaps less. There have been legendary figures in print journalism who, it has been said, could recall perfectly from memory every incident they witnessed and every conversation they had. Much radio has been no more than a broadcaster talking into a microphone. A reliable record, however, has always been regarded as the key to translating raw information into publishable and broadcastable material – and 'reliable' has been quantifiable in law.

The journalist's standard skill for note-taking has been shorthand. This has begun to go out of fashion, in part because of the availability of audio tape recorders, although most newspapers and many magazines and broadcasting organisations have continued to insist on it. All journalists have to some extent edited what they wrote, although particularly in print this has normally been regarded as a distinct skill. Radio journalists, however, have both recorded and edited tape, dubbed audio, recorded links and made packages as a matter of course, and television journalists have increasingly been required to have similar skills. All journalists have needed keyboard skills. Until relatively recently most of these skills overlapped only marginally with those required for the supposedly more technically oriented production processes in both print and broadcasting (although where the overlap actually occurred differed).

Developments in consumer electronics, most obviously in personal computing and video recording, but also in the ways in which access to advanced techniques has been made easier, have begun to blur the distinctions. Since the mid-1980s virtually every office in which journalists have worked has been computerised. Perhaps the majority of journalists have continued to use their personal computers (PCs) as glorified typewriters, and in many offices the designers (using Apple Macintoshes) have been distinguished from the writers and editors (using PCs). The trend, however, has been for journalists to acquire an expanding range of computing skills, covering not just word processing, but also data management, desk-top publishing, digital imaging, electronic editing, and design.

Writing

Without doubt the most valuable skill a journalist has been seen as possessing has been the ability to write. Even radio and television journalists, who have been rightly acknowledged for their verbal skills, have been dependent on scripting items, packages and bulletins. Moreover, there has been a strong inclination to stress the close relationship between fluency in writing and in speech. The NCTJ advised editors interviewing potential journalists that for those who 'can express themselves clearly in conversation' transferring 'their thoughts to paper should be a fairly easy operation'. Looking at it from the other angle, Ivor Yorke, a former head of journalist training for BBC news and current affairs, has insisted that 'It is taken for granted that *every* would-be journalist can write' (my emphasis).

Journalists have tended to focus on the mechanics of language in determining 'good' writing. This has been reinforced by recent panics over the supposed decline in literacy levels. While what many journalists have called 'flair' (or at least an acceptable, if not always wholly distinctive, style) has been regarded as desirable, clarity, conciseness and simplicity have been viewed as absolutely essential. Journalists have been expected to have a good grasp of standard spelling, punctuation, grammar and vocabulary: solecisms have been regarded with horror.

Under these headings of Personal qualities *and* Skills *should be listed two particularly important entries.*

Every journalist has been expected to come to terms with public exposure and scrutiny. Everything a journalist has written or recorded has been seen as entering the public domain, where it would be analysed, criticised, challenged and refuted. Journalists have been expected to be able to accept that their work will be subjected to this kind of open debate, starting with colleagues and managers. People who have found it difficult (or have not been prepared) to put their work on public display have normally struggled in journalism. Similarly, journalists have needed to be able to handle pressure. While pressure has taken many forms, arguably the most acute has been the pressure of deadlines, which have traditionally been absolute and ever-present. An essential skill for journalists has been to develop strategies for dealing with this constant pressure and for handling each deadline as it has arisen.

Knowledge

Almost all the knowledge that journalists have been expected to apply in their work has been of a general nature with a strong emphasis on a wide-ranging interest in (rather than deep understanding of) current affairs, and of the world in general. Journalists have stuck doggedly to the value of 'general knowledge'. The NCTJ has stressed that journalists should have 'an adequate background of *general* education' (my emphasis) which allows them 'to understand what is going on' around them.

Formally, the required minimum educational attainment has been unchanged since 1970 – five GCSEs. In practice, for at least a decade very few jobs have been open to people with fewer than two A-levels, and the number of recruits without A-levels has dwindled to a negligible figure. Trainees have not been accepted onto NCTJ pre-entry courses without two A-levels. The only stipulation made about subject areas has been that one qualification (either GCSE or A-level) was in English (Language). As the number of graduates has risen to more than 50 per cent of entrants to journalism, and this minimum requirement has not applied to them, new methods have had to be devised for establishing aptitudes for 'writing clear, concise English' (the NCTJ standard). This has most commonly involved university and college admissions tutors interviewing applicants for courses in much the same way as editors have done, and setting entry tests in written English.

The dedicated knowledge required of journalists has been acquired as part of their general training programme, and has been limited to law and public administration. Both have been approached as subjects to be learned, rather than analysed, and as being principally of practical use to journalists who have spent a large proportion of their working lives writing about politics and government in one form or another, and who need to know both how to cover the courts – and to keep out of them. The standard has been roughly speaking that of A-levels.

In 1993 trainee journalists began learning ethics as an 'underpinning knowledge' in the new NVQs in journalism. This reflected four trends: (i) the immediate concern with journalism standards (already noted); (ii) a general, government-led impetus in the 1980s towards 'reflective practice' in the professions (also referred to above); (iii) the inclusion of analytical elements as part of postgraduate vocational journalism courses in higher education from the 1970s; and (iv) the enormous expansion since the 1950s of critical academic media studies and related courses at all levels of education.

These developments ultimately made it imperative for journalism training to recognise more clearly the need for self-analysis and self-criticism. At the same time, however, they also highlighted another aspect of the uneasy relationship between journalism training and education: the question of the appropriateness of specific educational courses. This has been especially so in relation to media studies and related fields, which have generally been viewed antagonistically by journalists as 'too theoretical' and of no real practical use. Those providing such courses have stoutly defended their contribution to an overall growing critical awareness of the media, including journalism. Nevertheless, they have had to acknowledge that while their courses have proved attractive to students, neither the numbers of jobs available nor the qualities sought by media employers have closely matched the numbers and skills of emerging graduates. Media studies and related degrees and other awards have not been by themselves passports to employment in journalism.

Yet with more people entering journalism with degrees, and with the increased specialisation within journalism noted above, greater value has begun to be attached to wider knowledge and understanding. Specialist publications and broadcast areas recruiting entrants to journalism have been seeking out applicants with the relevant knowledge. An extreme example has been the consumer magazine publisher Future Publishing, which has made a point of hiring as journalists people with experience and knowledge of the subject area covered by the publication but who had no background in journalism. Similar situations have applied, although much more rarely, in general interest publications and programmes seeking specialist journalists. Nevertheless, this kind of knowledge has not yet widely become a primary factor in selection.

Traditionally, the personal qualities, skills and knowledge expected of a journalist have been general enough in practice to be seen as not presenting a bar to anyone wanting to enter journalism. Journalists, it has been commonly asserted, have come from more varied backgrounds than most professionals – and, it has been said, so it should be. Yet, despite this, stereotypes have persisted. Tyler's 'aspiring journalist' was a Cambridge politics graduate with a postgraduate award in journalism. A much-read authority on newspaper practice has written

> 'Today the young journalist will have done well in the arts side at school. He or she will have A-levels in such things as English, modern languages, history or economics, but will probably have shone at sports and group activities as well.'
>
> F. W. Hodgson
> *Modern Newspaper Practice* (Oxford, 1989)

Another has argued that 'a good general-purpose degree would be in English'. Journalism, according to a freelance who has taught aspiring journalists in adult education, has been 'too often thought of as something the talented just "do", like the arts'. This, and the large number of applicants for jobs and for places on both training and higher education courses, has no doubt been off-putting for many.

The attractions of 'being paid to see life, to travel and meet interesting, weird and important people' (Tyler) may have seemed so obvious that the large amount of mundane (but vitally important) routine work, often undertaken in small provincial towns, that has comprised journalism has been overlooked. The idea that journalism was for the high-flyers, the well-heeled and the well-connected has possibly been so pervasive that the efforts made to seek out and offer genuine rewards to those perceived above all to have ability have been unfairly discounted. However, it has to be admitted that the situation has been ambiguous. Nick Tomalin was sceptical about the 'type' to whom journalism appealed:

> 'The only qualities essential for real success in journalism are ratlike cunning, a plausible manner, and a little literary ability.
>
> The ratlike cunning is needed to ferret out and publish things that people don't want to be known . . .
>
> The plausible manner is useful for surviving while this is going on, helpful with the entertaining presentation of it . . . The literary ability is of obvious use. Other qualities are helpful, but not diagnostic.'
>
> *Sunday Times Magazine*
> (26 October 1969)

His observation may be read both ways, as indicating either the extent to which there has been no narrowly defined type to whom journalism was especially suited, or that the vagueness of the qualities sought in journalists has encouraged the colonisation of journalism by a small self-selecting group.

— Journalism – an exclusive club? —

'An argumentative, inquisitive, anarchistic and outrageous camaraderie of know-alls who claimed the right to be party to everything happening in the world that mattered a damn.'

Derek Jameson
Last of the Hot Metal Men (London, 1990)

This kind of description of Fleet Street in its hey-day reflects the extent to which journalism has been regarded as a kind of exclusive club. Arnold Wesker, who spent several months in 1971 in the offices of the *Sunday Times* gathering material for a play, and as an outsider was less admiring than Jameson, quoted one staffer as saying, 'Journalists write for other journalists, the people they have lunch with rather than the reader . . . they don't know what the reader thinks.' Wesker's own view was that 'Journalism may not be a secret activity but it is certainly one of the most "well protected"'. Like all clubs, it has had its rules of membership. Even if most journalists have seen themselves, as one who objected to Wesker's portrayal did, as 'very ordinary people doing reasonably well the only job they are capable of doing', they have not been terribly representative of society as a whole.

Journalism has been predominantly white and male. Overall, perhaps only about 30 per cent of British journalists in 1990 were women (see Table 4.1). Even in the USA the proportion of female journalists was no more than 34 per cent in 1992 (a figure that had not changed over a decade). The emphasis on news reporting as the chief mechanism for acquiring the necessary basic skills and experience as a journalist has been criticised for inculcating macho tendencies. Women have been excluded from the higher levels of journalism. By 1995 only two women were editing national newspapers, both Sunday tabloids, and only 16 per cent of those on the senior executive grade in the BBC were

JOURNALISM

♀ = Men
♀ = Women

[Bar chart showing percentages of men and women by sector:
- BOOKS: 30% men, 70% women
- BROADCASTING: 61% men, 39% women
- FREELANCE: 65% men, 35% women
- MAGAZINES: 54% men, 46% women
- NATIONAL PAPERS: 83% men, 17% women
- NATIONAL AGENCIES: 80% men, 20% women
- PUBLIC RELATIONS: 56% men, 44% women
- PROVINCIAL PAPERS: 71% men, 29% women
- TOTAL: 65% men, 35% women
- TOTAL UK: 65% men, 35% women
- TOTAL IRELAND: 67% men, 33% women
- RSI SUFFERERS: 40% men, 60% women]

Each whole symbol represents 10 per cent

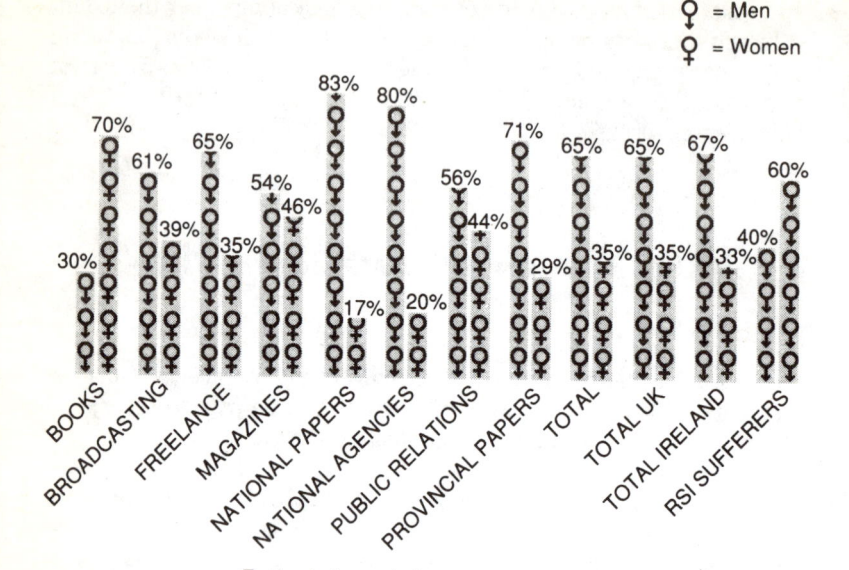

Table 4.1: Women in journalism: NUJ membership by sector. Source: National Union of Journalists (1994)

women. At the same time the number of women journalists in Britain has risen steadily, and by the early 1990s accounted for about 45 per cent of all entrants (in 1970 the figure was 25 per cent). They outnumbered men in many magazines, local radio stations and book publishing houses, and more than occasionally on local newspaper staffs. Even in these areas, however, where women editors and middle managers have been more common, female directors remained a rarity.

Black and Asian people have been grossly under-represented almost everywhere. A survey of newspapers in the east Midlands, where about 30 per cent of the general population has Asian and/or African origins, found only 3–4 per cent of journalists with such backgrounds. This has been recognised by, among others, the *Guardian*, BBC, *Sunday Times* and NCTJ: every university in the United Kingdom offering journalism courses has moved towards implementing an equal opportunities programme. Specific training, education, access and recruitment opportunities for 'ethnic minority' candidates have been introduced. There have been more long-standing opportunities for journalists with disabilities, although they have often been limited. There have been journalists with visual impairment and who use wheelchairs, and some effort has been made to recruit more.

More generally, the bias in favour of recruits with vaguely literary or arts backgrounds has resulted in poor numeracy and low levels of scientific and technological understanding in journalism. Those trained in science and technology have been increasingly in demand: at least one employer has identified his 'ideal' young journalist as a graduate in science *and* a modern language. Recognising these trends, postgraduate courses in journalism have also been accepting more students with such backgrounds, and acknowledging that some who pursue their interest in science and technology even as far as a doctorate may still enter journalism.

Journalists have commonly seen themselves as narrators, social observers and authors of the 'first draft of history'. They have paid much less attention to journalism as scientific investigation. One academic criticism of this approach has been that journalists cannot justify their belief in being 'passive observers of facts', and must acknowledge their role as 'active witnesses of happenings'. Recent developments in the media and related technology have served to highlight this. Satellite communications have made it possible for an audience almost anywhere in the world to see instantaneously what is happening almost anywhere-else. Television, particularly in the USA but also increasingly in Europe, has begun to rely on such 'real time' images. This has caused journalists to recognise that their traditional descriptions cannot compete with such coverage, and that what they have uniquely to offer is analysis, interpretation and commentary.

At the same time, the development in electronics has put at the disposal of journalists far more powerful tools for research. Although it has so far remained a marginal activity, some journalists (again with the Americans in the lead) have begun to exploit the access now available to enormous databanks, developing the necessary searching and interrogation skills, and acquiring the knowledge and understanding needed to make useful sense of multiple layers of information. Journalistic research has begun to move decisively away from the era of trawling through a pile of old clippings in a brown envelope.

Crucially, there has been a decline in demand for the basic product of journalism. Since 1945 the consumption of what might be called 'general news' has fallen steadily: this has occurred in both print and broadcasting. The problem has been seen as most acute in the local and regional press. The complete demise of this sector within the next ten years has been forecast: many long-established newspapers have already gone out of business. As part of an attempt to prevent this, newspaper companies have been in the vanguard in challenging many of the established notions of journalism. The largest provincial publishing group, Thomson Regional Newspapers (TRN) has argued that

> '. . . it is time to question the practices thought good enough in the past . . . We journalists are an arrogant bunch . . . [but] a radical reappraisal of what papers report and how they use their editorial manpower (*sic*) must be started, as a matter of urgency.'
> *The Key* (c.1990)

This type of approach, which became widespread in the 1990s, has shown three main characteristics: (i) a move away from the dominance of 'hard news'; (ii) the breaking down of demarcations among journalists between sub-editors, photographers, reporters, camera operators and designers; and (iii) a recognition in training and other practices of new dimensions of journalism skills and knowledge.

Journalism has been facing fundamental changes. The journalism weekly magazine *UK Press Gazette* has argued that many newspapers may soon provide 'something which few who have gone through the traditional journalistic training are ready or willing to give'. Therefore, it has become even more difficult to be prescriptive about the type of person who is likely to become a successful journalist. Recent changes in the media may be seen, however, as widening rather than narrowing opportunities. Journalism has begun to demand recruits with *both* more and varied skills, knowledge, understanding and aptitude, *and* the facility to continue learning throughout their working lives and to adapt to fundamental changes in working practices. The stereotypes of the past have been seen to be less applicable. Journalism has arguably become more open than it has been for some time.

5

—— MULTI-SKILLING ——

> 'We expect to see much greater interchange between the traditionally journalistic and technical roles in both news gathering and programme making.'
> David Gordon, chief executive,
> & Stewart Purvis, editor-in-chief,
> Independent Television News

> 'An all-purpose media worker will have confused priorities and never be able to perfect each one, if any.'
> Jack Mills, news editor/chief sub-editor,
> *Aldershot Courier* series

Journalism students have retained remarkably orthodox ambitions. A survey of her classmates on an NCTJ course in Portsmouth by trainee Elizabeth Hopkirk in 1992 revealed that the most favoured job was foreign correspondent, followed by newspaper or magazine editor and specialist writer. Many believed they would work in more than one medium, but that they would at least begin in newspapers (commonly before going into television). Such preferences reflected the patterns of journalism seemingly well established by the 1980s: movement between media (albeit usually *from* print *to* broadcasting), coupled with a high degree of specialism within both subject areas and the media themselves. There is ample evidence, however, that the system has been under considerable strain and may not survive the 1990s. What has often been referred to as 'a revolution' has been most advanced in provincial newspapers, where a number of large-scale experiments have begun in so-called 'multi-skilling' (and which by 1993 were beginning to be reflected in journalism training courses). Similar innovations have been introduced in broadcasting, especially the BBC's 'bi-media' scheme. Both advocates and opponents of such developments have argued that they signal at least 'radical change' (ITN's view) and possibly the demise of the 'traditional structure' of journalism (Westminster Press). So far, multi-skilling has taken a number of forms.

Newspapers

The main thrust of multi-skilling in newspapers has been to utilise computer technology to attempt to create a 'seamless' operation involving writers, sub-editors and designers. This has been based on the fact that stories are written directly into the computer systems from which the finished newspaper will emerge for printing (known as 'single keystroking'). Why, the argument has gone, should a reporter write a story on one terminal for it to be sub-edited on a second terminal to fit a page lay-out designed on a third terminal, and with the people involved rarely, if ever, communicating directly even though they are all working on the same electronic system? Why not link up the people? Moreover, by separating the tasks in the traditional way there is both more opportunity to get things wrong and less individual job satisfaction. This has been the philosophy behind TRN's 'Project Key'. Its booklet, *The Key*, argued

> 'Most newsrooms are similar to the old Ford production line . . . a reporter writes copy, passes to newsdesk; news editor checks it, sends to chief sub; chief sub "tastes" it, delegates to page planner; page planner schemes it, gives to a sub; sub-editor subs it and sends it to outputter. It's old-fashioned, clumsy, it wastes time and it puts creativity and initiative on the spike.'

TRN's answer was WED ('the wedding of Writing, Editing and Design') formulated around 'integrated teams' of news editors, picture editors and sub-editors, and of journalists, photographers and designers, which 'must blur the edges – tear down old fences'. One early, if limited, implementation of the new philosophy was the abolition of separate news and features editorships on papers such as the *Journal* in Newcastle and *Press and Journal* in Aberdeen, and the creation of a new all-embracing post of head of content. What TRN designated 'WED-style command desks' were established on papers such as the *Belfast Telegraph*.

A similar approach appeared to be carried further in various experiments set up by papers in the Westminster Press group. At the *Evening Echo* in Basildon 'multi-functional teams' of sub-editors and reporters were established to see projects through from the initial idea to the point where the finished article was sent for printing. At the Brighton *Evening Argus* reporters, photographers and sub-editors were teamed up with each expected to be able to do the others' jobs as well as their own. Mark Ashley, managing director of Lancashire Publications, asked in 1993,

> 'Why do we have to have photographers? Why can't we get journalists who sub one week, do crown court the next and sport the next . . . ?'

Such arrangements have been tried less in national newspaper offices, although *The Independent* was launched in 1986 with integrated news and sub-editors desks 'to get away from the us and them syndrome', and in March 1994 the *Daily Mirror* introduced teams of sub-editors and designers working on specific sections or pages of the paper as a precursor to a multi-skilling initiative throughout Mirror Group Newspapers.

The major effect of these experiments has probably been to challenge what Brian Page, the assistant editor of Westminster Press' *Northern Echo*, decried as the 'traditionally hide-bound and compartmentalised' structures of journalism which kept writers (often physically) apart from sub-editors; made fundamental distinctions between reporters and photographers, and established complex and steep editorial hierarchies (see Figure 5.1). In February 1994 the *Telegraph and Argus* in Bradford (also a Westminster Press newspaper) introduced an 'orbital' newsroom, with teams of sub-editors, reporters and specialist writers; physical integration, and a flatter editorial hierarchy. The scheme was based on the NEWSworks system developed by the city desk editor of a paper in Burlington, Vermont, and piloted by the Gannett Newspaper Division.

Broadcasting

Radio and television have been slower to take up multi-skilling. It was preceded by bi-media working at the BBC, in which journalists have worked for both television and radio. By May 1993 there were more than 50 bi-media correspondents, supported by bi-media editors,

JOURNALISM

TRADITIONAL NEWSROOM

THE 'ORBITAL' NEWSROOM
The new-style newsroom at the *Telegraph & Argus* in Bradford

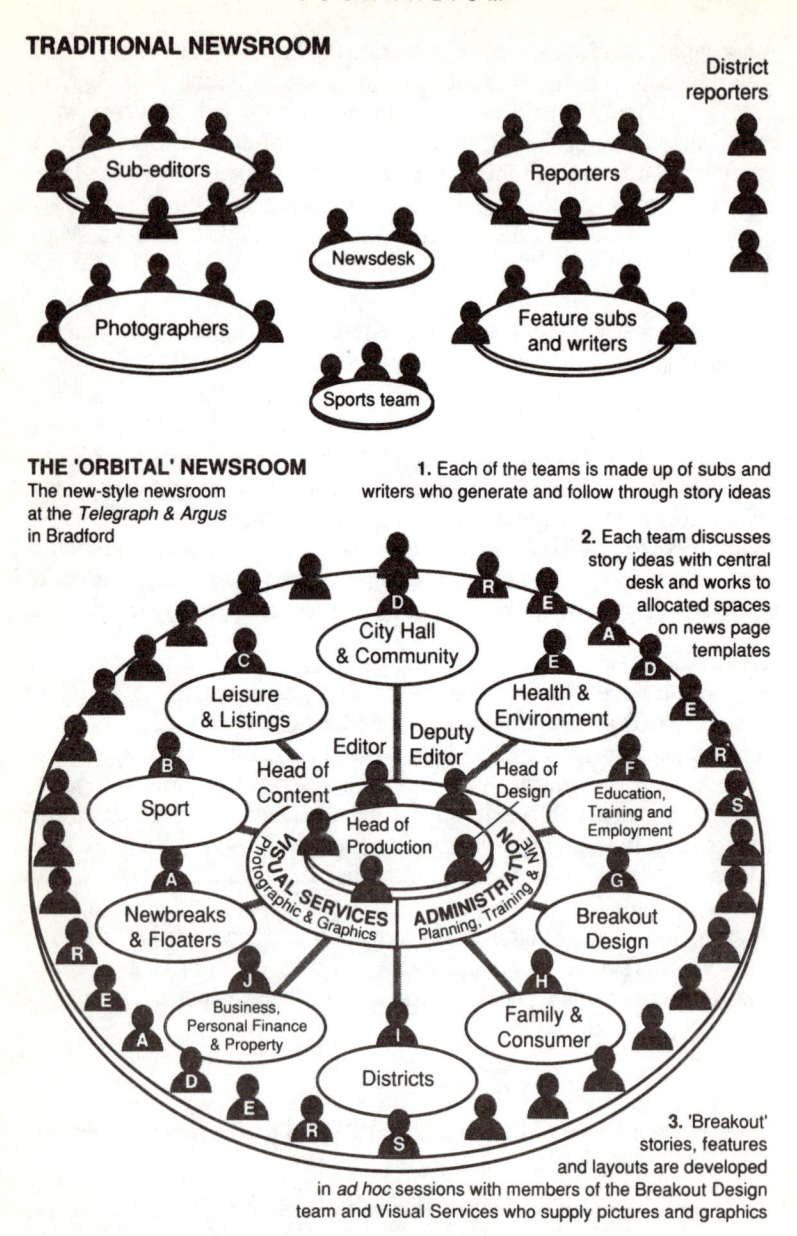

1. Each of the teams is made up of subs and writers who generate and follow through story ideas

2. Each team discusses story ideas with central desk and works to allocated spaces on news page templates

3. 'Breakout' stories, features and layouts are developed in *ad hoc* sessions with members of the Breakout Design team and Visual Services who supply pictures and graphics

Figure 5.1: The standard editorial structure for an average sized newspaper, and the 'orbital' newsroom introduced at the Bradford *Telegraph and Argus*.
Source: Westminster Press

operating in all the regional centres of the Corporation. The scheme was confined initially to journalists covering business, industry and local government, and later health, education and the environment. It was seen that while tapping into the analysis of a specialist by a number of television programmes and radio stations was viable, trying to share coverage of fast-moving news stories was less likely to work satisfactorily. A major argument for introducing the practice was the need to abolish the duplication involved in a great deal of the BBC's journalism, where reporters from several programmes and stations would cover the same story. One of the busiest bi-media correspondents, based in Leeds, ended up working for three television regions and ten radio stations. Other advantages have been claimed for the system, however: that it has concentrated resources so that bi-media specialists have had more time to develop stories, and that generally there has been more co-ordination of effort between various BBC programmes and stations. Some specialist correspondents in the BBC's national news and current affairs department have been trained in bi-media work, and the practice looked like being adopted in other broadcasting organisations: HTV Wales entered into a bi-media agreement with Marcher Coast FM radio in north Wales in 1993.

The next step in broadcasting has been closer to genuine multi-skilling. The BBC attempted to introduce within the space of two years the practice of journalists carrying camcorders to shoot their own video footage. The first journalists equipped with the cameras in 1992 were foreign correspondents working for World Service Television. A few months later, the Corporation proposed that more than 1,000 regional radio reporters in the United Kingdom should use camcorders to shoot footage for television before regular camera crews arrived on stories. The objective was to introduce the practice to national news and current affairs as well by 1994. What has been called 'video reporting', in which journalists can even film themselves talking to camera, was started by cable television companies in America, and a British cable channel, operated by Associated Newspapers and due on air in 1994, proposed to equip up to 50 journalists with camcorders. The BBC experiment, however, faced opposition from journalists (see below). Nevertheless, the BBC's commitment to broaden the skills of its journalists seemed real. According to Chris Cramer, head of BBC news gathering, 'In five or six years time . . . it will be as natural for a correspondent abroad to pick up a camera as to pick up a Biro.' Meanwhile, experiments in full multi-skilling were going ahead. At the BBC's Westminster studios, reporters have been trained in tape editing and handling camera equipment, and camera operators have been taught journalism. At the beginning of 1994 ITN also proposed to train journalists in tape editing and video library skills, while directors would learn how to write.

As in newspapers, one effect has been to break down the barriers between journalists and, in this case, technicians. Flatter news room hierarchies also seemed likely to emerge. Both the BBC and ITN had plans to lessen the occupational gradations between researchers and journalists by introducing the new grades, respectively, of broadcast assistants and news assistants. BBC radio and television news was also unified under a single head of news programmes covering both media.

UK Press Gazette pointed out that there was in fact relatively little new in multi-skilling. Many, possibly most, journalists were already used to developing a range of skills founded on basic news reporting: writing and editing, research and directing camera crews, recording and editing audio tape. Freelances and some staff journalists on small magazines have traditionally taken photographs to illustrate their own stories. Supporters of multi-skilling have argued that it improves journalism by giving journalists more complete control over their work. Those in opposition, however, claimed that it represented an attack on the specific and highly developed skills of writing, taking pictures, editing, etc, and would replace them with an unfocused generalism – 'making a member of staff a Jack-of-all-trades rather than a master of one', according to one group of newspaper journalists.

Journalists have generally viewed multi-skilling with suspicion. The NUJ has condemned what it calls 'a superficial exercise' as one of a number of changes which 'point clearly to the downgrading in importance of the editorial content of newspapers', and in June 1993 BBC Television NUJ members voted 9-to-1 against using camcorders largely because the practice was seen as undermining their role as journalists. The MP Malcolm Bruce argued in a House of Commons debate

> 'The press – regional and national – have undermined the drive towards accuracy by forcing [the] experienced out of jobs in favour of cheap, inefficient and untrained journalists in order to bring down costs and, with them, standards.'

There has been less opposition to bi-media working. One explanation for this might be that the introduction of bi-media journalism has not been associated as much with more general attempts to cut editorial costs. 'We can demonstrate,' *UK Press Gazette* editorialised in January

1994, '. . . that multi-skilling itself is not the problem.' Even opponents of existing schemes, such as Jack Mills, have recognised the value of the 'legitimate multi-skilling of genuine creative and product-improving intent'. There can be little doubt that both newspapers and broadcasting have been motivated chiefly by commercial pressures in the form of increased competition within static or declining markets, and this has led to fundamental reappraisals of the role and practices of journalists.

Some changes in journalism practices were already under way, however, before the advent of experiments in multi-skilling. These included a move away from the coverage of politics, international affairs and other public matters in favour of more concentration on the private lives of celebrities, the stars of television soaps and the Royal Family. There was less concern with the 'truth': *The Sun* ran a story claiming that the Princess Royal was expecting a child, based on a poll of its own readers in which a majority said they *thought* she was pregnant. The rigours of checking the authenticity of stories seemed to be less well observed. In one case it was alleged that *The Sun* accepted and printed without making further checks a story about the affair between the Conservative Cabinet Minister David Mellor and the actress Antonia de Sancha which had been invented by a publicity agent. The journalist Wensley Clarkson revealed in his book *Dog Eat Dog* (1990) that the secret of successful tabloid journalism was not to pursue a story to its logical conclusion but to satisfy the editorial executives by producing the material they required.

Although these developments were associated mainly with the tabloid national press and particularly *The Sun*, they emerged, too, in the provincial press. Many regional newspapers attempted to emulate the circulation successes of *The Sun* by imitating its approach. A commentator in the *Daily Telegraph* condemned them for 'scrap[ing] the barrel for sensational news stories'. Such journalism appeared to be produced to formulae, reducing the initiative, imagination, curiosity and ingenuity expected of journalists. Estimates varied, but it was generally agreed that between two-thirds and four-fifths of local and regional newspaper news originated from official sources, such as the police, the courts and local authorities. More and more journalism was conducted over the telephone from editorial offices located on industrial estates. Journalists said they spent between 60 and 90 per cent of their working day in their offices. In 1991 John Tusa, managing director of the BBC World Service, referred to a prophesy made in 1965 by the former journalist Michael Frayn in his novel *The Tin Men* that newspaper stories could be produced by computer. That situation had almost arrived, he said. In 1993 Michael Grade, the chief executive of Channel 4, criticised television current affairs for being 'sound-alike, look-alike, anonymous', and the products of 'carefully homogenised and processed script[s]'. Programmes, he said,

> '... all feel as if they have been created on some journalistic, electronic mass production line.'
>
> *UK Press Gazette* (24 May 1993)

Even the centrality of 'good English' appeared to be challenged. On many local radio stations journalists were no longer required to write scripts, and conventional spelling and grammar were considered unimportant. One (short-lived) newspaper unilaterally abolished the apostrophe. What had appeared to be the established virtues of journalism were perhaps becoming optional extras.

The future

It seemed impossible to project with any certainty the shape of journalism through the 1990s. In 1994 the Guild of Editors asked the Centre of Journalism Studies at Cardiff to conduct a survey of training needs in the provincial press. Earlier research by the University of Central Lancashire stressed the need 'to develop the skills and knowledge of all staff so that each member is able to operate in a multi-skilled and team-based work environment' (*The Changing Vision*, 1993). Journalists, it was argued, had to be more integrated into 'overall newspaper strategies', particularly the identification of target audiences. Indeed, journalists joining one paper in the North West of England spent part of their first week in a newsagent's shop. The deputy editor of a series of weekly papers told the researchers,

> 'Journalists are becoming more newspaper people. They are going to take a much wider role in the whole industry. We need a much wider training programme. Journalists are information seekers. There is a growing awareness that there is a great benefit in getting journalists involved in the company.'

The research report identified a need to change 'ingrained habits'. The BBC and ITN have both emphasised what they see as the longer-term advantages of greater flexibility among journalists, and have undertaken to concentrate investment in training on journalists who 'have the aptitude and attitude to adapt' (ITN). At the Essex County Newspapers group journalists, including the editor of the *Halstead Gazette and Advertiser*, volunteered in 1992 to sell advertising. The notion was greeted with outrage by journalists elsewhere. The editor of the group's *Colchester Evening Gazette*, Martin McNeill, defended the scheme, arguing, 'I wouldn't put my staff in a position where their professional role would be compromised'.

Part of the impetus for change has arisen as a result of developments in technology. As has already been noted, journalists have access to electronic systems which have simplified (or even by-passed) the work previously done by technical specialists such as typesetters, film editors and designers. Those systems have also been made directly accessible from remote and mobile stations. This has resulted in an explosion of 'real time' news coverage. On a less spectacular level, combined with the casualisation of journalism, it has led to more journalists working from home, linked computer-to-computer to the media via telecommunications (often called 'teleworking'). Such electronic networking has also assisted in linking journalists to new sources of information. It has been predicted that, taken together, these developments will compel journalists to reassess the ways in which they work; for example, Peter Chapman, who has considerable experience of provincial newspapers, condemned the fact that

'Journalists get no proper training in electronic information networks. There is no place on the training scheme for modern research input. They are just being trained in the old journalism skills.'

Such concerns have also reflected external changes occurring outside the news media. In the 1980s, as computers became widely available, tens of millions of non-journalists gained shared or exclusive access to most of the same type of equipment, applications and data used in journalism. A proliferation of desk-top publishing packages and the emergence of international computer networks encouraged new forms of communication and production. By the early 1990s there were more village newsletters published in Britain than newspapers. Electronic bulletin boards threatened to multiply at an even faster rate. The international network Internet remained a 'global experiment', but had already made thousands of electronic texts (etexts) available: the California-based Project Gutenberg proposed to distribute one trillion etext files by the year 2001. Many apparently wild claims were made for the hardware to handle these volumes of data. Nevertheless, major media companies, such as ITN and News International, seemed seriously committed to what the *Times* called 'the brave new media world'. The projected realisation of the potential of unlimited global communication gave rise to notions of the 'information rich society', of 'data superhighways' and of 'communicopia'. David Gordon, the chief executive of ITN, has forecast the development of 'the global teleputing village', in which (digitalised) news would be available on demand and in forms determined by members of the audience. Experiments in interactive media began in Britain in the 1990s with a television shopping channel, and cable TV viewers being able to recall video replays of soccer matches.

What seemed to connect all these developments was visual attraction. Research carried out for TRN revealed that artwork and photographs attracted the attention of newspaper readers more than three times as much as text. Many newspapers concentrated a great deal of effort on carrying advanced graphics, made possible again by the availability of computers. TRN has urged that graphics people 'should be treated as reporters – who happen to draw or illustrate the story rather than write it.' Ultimately, it has been forecast, newspapers will be published on screen: at least two companies were intending to launch portable, notebook sized, computerised receivers (called personal digital assistants) by the end of the 1990s.

One analysis of these trends has been that media power will shift from the producer (the journalist) to the consumer (the audience). The ability of the consumer to exercise choice, it has been argued, will encourage more people to produce. This in turn will drive down costs, leading to more choice. The technology has been developed to carry literally limitless amounts of information. Andrew Knight, executive chairman of News International, argued in 1993 that

'The explosion of choice puts you, the consumer, in the driving seat . . . When choice and medium (*sic*) are multiplying at such impossible pace, nobody could dominate what you read or see.'
*A British Success Story:
An Examination of Prospects
for the UK Media*

MULTI-SKILLING

Figure 5.2: New technology in journalism. ITN's Desktop News System transmits television news video via satellite to computers.
Source: Independent Television News

Going even further, Knight's boss, Rupert Murdoch, predicted that 'Anybody will be able to start media, or get anything they want for the price of a phone call. The days of the media baron are over.'

Subsequently he was accused of being disingenuous; of cultivating 'the image of . . . the non-tycoon' while retaining control over a vast and expanding media empire. Another critique has been that this future contains, as well as information wealth, for those without the resources the prospects of information poverty; that the bulk of the new channels of communication will be dedicated to revenue-raising mass entertainment – and information will come at a premium price. Power, access and cheapness, Gordon has argued, will lead to further tabloidisation and 'newsotainment' (Gordon's word for infotainment). Murdoch's views, however, have received a measure of support from Bill Gates, the head of the software manufacturer, Microsoft, who has proposed information technology as a democratising force, leading to individual liberation and empowerment. George Gilder, of the Discovery Institute, whose work influenced US government policy, asserted that telecomputing would

> '. . . blow apart all the monopolies, hierarchies, pyramids and power grids of established industrial society . . . All hierarchies will tend to become "heterarchies" – systems in which each individual rules his (*sic*) own domain. In contrast to a hierarchy ruled from the top, a heterarchy is a society of equals under the law.'
> *Life After Television* (1992)

The arguments have by no means been conclusive, and it has not been clear where the journalist will stand in all this. Some, like the experienced foreign correspondents Robert Fisk, of *The Independent*, and Mort Rosenblum, of Associated Press, claimed that by the early 1990s analytical, interpretive and investigative journalism had already been effectively driven from television and the 'popular' press. Others, including Gordon, argued that 'The editorial process, the exercise of news judgement, the editing and presentational skills' would become valuable commodities as audiences tried to make sense of the bombardment of information to which they were subjected. The indications, however, were that the journalists of the 1990s would be expected to rely progressively less on their traditional specific skills, intuitive approach and wayward creativity, and to develop greater strategic awareness and all-round knowledge and understanding.

6

THE MEDIA

> 'At long last we are starting to produce a newspaper for readers instead of journalists.'
> Perry Austin-Clark, editor, *Telegraph and Argus*, Bradford

> 'We have to make choices and that rests around stories being important and significant rather than interesting.'
> Mark Damazer, editor, BBC TV news programmes

National and provincial press

By the 1990s the media in Britain were undergoing the kind of fundamental change which last occurred about 100 years earlier when modern mass communications were established. The major effect was a growing inter-connection between different media, usually within large transnational corporations, and known in the media industries as 'synergy'. This resulted in concentrations of ownership and power which were seen by many critics as worrying. Such developments were by no means new in the 1990s, however: many of the characteristics of the contemporary media industries had begun to emerge at least 30 years previously. It was commonplace to hold up Rupert Murdoch and his print, broadcasting, publishing and film interests (in the USA, Britain, the Pacific Rim and Australia) as the archetype of late twentieth century global media imperialism. Yet as early as the 1950s Roy (later Lord) Thomson, a Canadian, began assembling multi-national, multi-media holdings which by the 1970s included a presence in Canada, the USA, Africa and the United Kingdom, and control of newspapers, television, radio, book publishing and magazines. In the United Kingdom Thomson owned the *Times* and *Sunday Times*; the largest group of provincial newspapers (including the *Scotsman, Western Mail* and *Belfast Telegraph*); Scottish Television (which, he claimed, amounted to 'a licence to print money'); a chain of magazines; Yellow Pages, and publishers such as Sphere, Michael Joseph and Hamish Hamilton, as well as the largest holiday company in Britain. The question was whether there was something essentially different about the changes which occurred during the 1980s and into the 1990s.

By the 1960s the personally powerful 'media baron' typified by Harmsworth and Lord Beaverbrook (the owner of the *Daily Express*, who said, 'I run my paper purely for the purpose of making propaganda and for no other purpose') had effectively disappeared. There is no doubt that with the emergence of Thomson and later Murdoch the *image* of the media baron survived. Neither, however, was a simple propagandist. Unlike Harmsworth or Beaverbrook, the new media owners' personal ambitions were circumscribed by the complexities of contemporary corporate finances, in which shareholders and banks exercised powerful voices: Thomson and Murdoch were both businessmen who happened to be newspaper publishers, and their emergence reflected changes in the media markets.

For most of the 100 years after the establishment of the mass circulation newspaper industry in the 1880s, the national press had dominated the media in the United Kingdom. News was the press' prime product, and newspaper production was geared to getting the most comprehensive, most up-to-date and, where possible, exclusive coverage to the readers. The main concern of newspaper publishers was to secure supplies of the raw materials, labour, and journalism which made up their papers. To this end, publishers invested *vertically* in the industry: for example, in paper makers (Mirror Group Newspapers owned 44 per cent of the Reed paper group); in machinery manufacturers (several newspapers had shares in the Linotype company which produced typesetting equipment); in purpose-built newspaper offices (giving rise to the location of the national newspaper industry in Fleet Street), and in staff (particularly journalists who were taken on in their thousands). By the 1960s, however, such investment was providing meagre, if any, returns: the national press was notoriously unprofitable, and control of more than one (or two) newspapers or (after 1955) independent television companies was restricted by anti-monopoly regulation.

Thomson believed he could extract satisfactory profits from the media by introducing the modern management techniques, principles of marketing and latest technology which, it was argued, the old-fashioned press barons had eschewed, but which he had already introduced in his Canadian newspapers. Thomson set about 'modernising' the provincial press through rationalisation, chiefly by building the largest provincial publishing group in the United Kingdom, and introducing economies of scale and uniformity. He simultaneously succeeded and failed. Thomson's career highlighted both the centrality of the market in media development in the period from 1960, and the important relationship of the market to technology. While Thomson, using 'modern' business methods, was able to exploit a largely traditional provincial newspaper market, attempts at more radical changes, chiefly through the introduction of 'new technology' (notably at the *Times* and *Sunday Times* in the 1970s) failed.

Elsewhere in the national newspaper industry the most noticeable change was the movement of readers away from the middle market press (the *Daily Mail, Daily Express*) to the tabloids. Between 1965 and 1980 the tabloids' share of national newspaper readerships rose from 38 per cent to 56 per cent. This quite dramatic shift was accounted for, however, by one factor: the sale by the International Publishing Corporation (IPC) to Murdoch of the middle market *Sun* in 1969, and its subsequent relaunch as a tabloid paper. The national newspaper industry was in long-term decline. Total circulations reached something near their peak in 1957 at 45.8m (16.7m dailies and 29.1m Sundays). By 1979 they were down to 34.5m (15.2m dailies and 19.3m Sundays), falls of 25 per cent in total circulations; 9 per cent among the dailies, and 34 per cent for the Sundays.

One consequence of this appeared to be the quite dramatic closure of a large number of papers. Of the eight titles which ceased publication between 1960 and 1971, five folded during a 12-month period in 1960–61. The story was not one of simple contraction, but rather of reorganisation and repositioning. Mergers (sometimes accompanied by changes in ownership) betokened rationalisation: the *News Chronicle* and *Daily Sketch* were both merged into the *Daily Mail* (in 1960 and 1971 respectively); the *Sunday Dispatch* with the *Sunday Express* (1961); the

London evening newspaper *The Star* with the *Evening News* (1960). At least two papers (the *Sunday Graphic* and *Sunday Chronicle*) were closed so that their printing presses could be more profitably leased to other newspapers. Publication was further concentrated in London, the *Manchester Guardian* (with a suitable change of title) moving in 1961 and the *Empire News* (also Manchester based) closing in 1960. The only new papers to appear (the *Sunday Telegraph* in 1961, and the *Daily Star* in 1978) were launched to utilise the spare printing capacity of existing titles (the *Daily Telegraph* and *Daily Express* respectively). This latter move by itself indicated the complex manœuverings which were going on, as the *Daily Star* was started, against the long-term trend, specifically to use spare printing capacity in Manchester.

There were also relaunches: the *Sunday Pictorial* as the *Sunday Mirror* (1963); *Reynold's News* (*Sunday Citizen* – 1962); and the *Daily Herald* as *The Sun* (in 1965, before being sold to Murdoch). This single transformation reflected the wider adoption of the tabloid format: before 1962 there had been only three tabloid newspapers, but in the following 16 years six papers either converted or were launched as tabloids. All the biggest selling newspapers (the *Daily* and *Sunday Mirror*, *People*, *Daily Express* and *The Sun*) were being published in tabloid format by 1977 with the exception of the *Sunday Express* and *News of the World*. The newspapers that closed had readerships totalling about eight million, and their demise could not have been a straightforward reflection of declining circulations.

The net result of all this activity was that during three relatively short periods, a large part of the national press underwent some kind of change. The first occurred between 1959 and 1961, when five dailies and six Sundays were affected; the second in 1969–71 (three dailies and three Sundays), and, finally, in 1976 and 1977 (two Sundays, a daily and the London *Evening Standard*). In circulation terms about 60 per cent of the lost newspapers were in the middle market. As well as the changes already noted, new patterns of ownership emerged. The significant newcomers were Thomson (*The Times* and *Sunday Times*), Murdoch (*News of the World* and *The Sun*), and Trafalgar House (*Daily* and *Sunday Express* and *Daily Star*), although Pearson/Westminster Press who bought the *Financial Times* in 1957 might be added to the list. Taken together, these factors suggested that the fashionable business practices of the time (known variously as rationalisation, streamlining, and modernisation) were being deployed (often by newcomers to the industry) in an attempt to turn the traditional press into profitability.

As a mature industry, the national press suffered from high costs, made worse by a rapid rise in the cost of paper (newsprint). Almost all the new owners targeted costs, and particularly labour costs (which the Royal Commission on the Press in 1977 found accounted for between 40 and 50 per cent of the total). Technologies available in the 1970s offered opportunities to cut labour costs by replacing much of the production work done manually with automated electronic systems. The national press, however, did not generally take them up. A wide-ranging agreement was reached with the main print unions in the mid-1970s to introduce so-called new technology throughout Fleet Street, but it was subsequently rejected by the unions' members. Individual attempts by Times Newspapers (noted above) and the Mirror Group to go over to new systems were also frustrated (the former after a year-long lock-out). Thus, it became commonplace to blame trade union intransigence, made effective by strong workplace organisation and militancy, for the failure to adopt labour-saving technology. Some culpability was also placed at the door of newspaper managements, who were said to be too ineffectual. Nevertheless, given the nature of the changes which occurred in the 1960s and 1970s (and the fact that newspapers remained comparatively cheap), it may fairly be asked whether it was felt that the national newspaper industry needed to pay greater attention to satisfying its existing markets than to embarking on technical innovation.

The provincial press was certainly more innovative in this respect; but then it was also believed to be in a more parlous state. A quarter of the regional morning newspapers (six out of 26) closed between 1955 and 1963. In the 1960s at least eight major cities lost evening papers, and between 1961 and 1974 there was a net loss of about 100 weeklies. As with the national press, however, the issue was not one of a crude decline in readers: not only did evening newspaper circulations remain more or less steady at around 6.5 million, but more than a dozen new evening papers were launched in the 1960s and 1970s. (Morning newspaper circulations also held up at around 2 million.) What was changing was the market. Provincial newspapers had been traditionally clustered in geographical centres where there was more often than not more than one type of paper (morning, evening and weekly) and sometimes even a choice between two or more evening, weekly and (more rarely) morning papers. In addition to this internal competition, the provincial press had to compete with the national newspapers (morning papers), the BBC, independent television from 1955, and independent local radio (ILR) from 1973. In short, the market became increasingly crowded.

The industry's response was to rationalise the distribution of titles: the number of competing provincial papers was reduced until only Glasgow and Belfast had two morning papers and by 1980 no town or city (including London) had more than one evening paper. A third of towns with more than one weekly paper in 1961 were reduced to a single title by 1974. The number of towns with a morning and an evening newspaper declined more slowly; but increasingly the two papers were owned by the same company. This indicated the mechanism chosen to introduce the rationalisation of the provincial press: the concentration of ownership within both national and regional chains.

The basic pattern of ownership had been set in the 1930s, and the only major change came when Thomson bought out the Kemsley interests in 1959. The other national groups, Northcliffe/Associated, Westminster Press and United Provincial and the provincial groups (those owning newspapers in one or two specific areas, rather than a chain spread nationally) had established their presence before the Second World War. These groups began to consolidate their interests in the 1960s chiefly by acquiring, often from each other, more titles in the same (or neighbouring) towns. They looked to own not only perhaps the morning and evening papers (as Thomson did in Aberdeen, Cardiff, Newcastle and Edinburgh), but also the urban and rural weeklies. Such concentrations offered the advantages of economies of scale, joint production and uniform advertising sales. As has been noted earlier, Thomson in particular applied marketing and sales techniques imported from north America.

Insofar as these activities were confined to an attempt to rationalise the existing press, there appeared to be little need to apply more radical remedies. The development of new evening newspapers, however, provided more incentives to introduce 'new technology'. Thomson, who played a lead role, used the opportunity presented by the establishment of 'green field' papers in Reading and Hemel Hempstead to experiment with photo-composition, and to change to web offset printing. The 'new technology' was generally introduced slowly and without significant upheaval. A small number of newspapers, most notably the *Nottingham Evening Post* and the *Express and Star*, Wolverhampton, made early and perhaps more adventurous forays into computing, and the new techniques had obvious appeal to those offering contract printing. The creation of what the chairman of one provincial newspaper group called 'monopolies, or near monopolies . . . shrewdly constructed' in the 1960s was a far greater disincentive, however.

By the late 1970s that situation had begun to change with the emergence of the free weekly paper. In 1975 there were 185 so-called freesheets; in 1980 the figure had risen to 325. By 1979 significant free newspaper publishers, led by the Yellow Advertiser Group, had been established. What made the phenomenon possible, according to Frank Branson, a former weekly newspaper reporter who started the free *Bedfordshire on Sunday* with less than £10,000 in 1977, was the decline in printing costs resulting from the introduction of computerisation and the fall in editorial standards of the established papers. 'They got too big, too bureaucratic and too greedy,' he later wrote. All the same, these established papers saw little to fear in the new development.

Television and radio

In television and radio, too, there was some repositioning without a fundamental restructuring of the system. That remained based on an overriding commitment to public service broadcasting expressed not only in the institutionalisation of the BBC but also in the regulations governing independent television (started in 1955). The regional commercial stations effectively monopolised commercial television in their areas, and the network system resulted in the four (after 1968, five) largest sharing access uncompetitively. In the three reviews of ITV franchises conducted in 1964, 1967 and 1981, only nine adjustments were made to what were originally 15 franchises. These included the addition of breakfast television in 1982, and the division of the Northern region in 1968. In total, out of a possible 51 opportunities to withdraw franchises, that sanction was exercised fully only four times. Commercialism was still regarded as a crass intrusion into broadcasting, and as a kind of counter the BBC was given the so-called third channel: BBC2 began transmitting in 1964.

Initially, much of the change in television simply by-passed radio. Then in 1964 the BBC's monopoly was challenged by unlawful broadcasts from off-shore stations romantically called 'pirate radio'. The response, again, was to make adjustments which fell short of radical surgery. In 1967, the BBC reorganised its national output into Radios 1, 2, 3 and 4, and introduced local radio broadcasting. This was significant in two ways: first, the idea which had permeated the BBC since its foundation that all programming should be mixed and not specialised was abandoned; and, second, there was a weakening of the Corporation's high degree of centralisation in London. It was a further seven years before the first commercial independent local radio (ILR) stations were licensed; but, while they relied on advertising, organisationally they, too, followed the BBC model. These stations were relatively large and served areas of high population, starting naturally in London (the first on air were LBC and Capital). The costs of setting up an ILR station were also high, and, led by the example of the BBC, there was a reluctance to crowd the airwaves, especially as the United Kingdom had limited numbers of available wavelengths. Some of the biggest investors in ILR were newspapers, with shares of up to 50 per cent of one station (in Reading), and between 20 and 25 per cent of most.

Magazines

As might be expected, changes in the magazine industry broadly speaking followed the pattern of conglomeration, transnationalism, cross-media integration and marketing innovation described above. Between 1958 and 1961 International Publishing Corporation (IPC), which also had interests in newspapers (the Mirror Group) and television, emerged as the dominant force in magazines. In the 1960s, American ideas (and in the 1970s, American publishers, who had been present in the UK market since the beginning of the century) began to exert considerable influence. Two US companies in particular, National Magazines and Conde Nast, launched a number of titles – *Harpers and Queen* (1970), *Cosmopolitan* (1972), *Company* (1978). IPC tried in the 1960s to 'Americanise' some of its women's magazines. This was in response to a changing market. The 1950s had been the hey-day of the women's weekly magazines, but they were hit by the introduction of commercial television. Almost immediately, these magazines lost about a third of their advertising.

At the beginning of the 1960s the broadsheet Sunday newspapers began to produce their own colour magazines as supplements: the first appeared with the *Sunday Times* in 1962. A further third of the advertising of the mass circulation weekly magazines disappeared in the 1970s. Yet three major women's weekly titles had been launched in the late 1950s – *Woman's Mirror* (1955), *Woman's Day* (1958) and *Woman's*

Realm (also 1958). Not surprisingly, the first two failed to survive the 1960s. The women's weeklies were under attack from three directions:

- the age and class profile of their market was changing, from older middle-class to younger working-class readers;
- general interest magazines as a whole were in decline with titles such as *Reveille* and *Titbits* also struggling, and the two listings magazines, *Radio Times* and *TV Times* achieving their peak joint circulation in 1960 followed by a steep decline to 1971; and,
- the more specialised and closely targeted magazines tended to be published monthly rather than weekly.

Efforts were made to address the new readers with titles such as *Honey* (1960), *Jackie* (1963) and *19* (1968) for younger women; *Family Circle* (1964) and *Living* (1967) which focused on women's roles in the home; and *Women's World* (1977). In the 1970s both *Woman's Own* and *Woman* changed their editorial policies, becoming more feminist and 'modern'. The decade, however, belonged to monthly titles (all the 1970s magazines listed above, except *Jackie*, were published monthly). Between 1957 and 1978 the five top-selling weeklies lost nearly three million readers (or a third of their aggregate circulations). By comparison, eight monthly titles launched during the 1970s had together accumulated nearly 2.7 million new readers.

None of these monthly magazines had an individual circulation approaching 1 million, while three of the weeklies were each still selling around 1.5 million copies. One of the main characteristics of the period was the division of magazines into mass circulation and smaller, segmented circulation titles, and the growth in numbers of the latter. This arose in part as a result of the combined effects of television, which (as noted above) attracted an increasing percentage of the available advertising, and newspapers whose editorial coverage concentrated less on news and more on features, gossip, Royals-watching and television programme listings. Nevertheless, television offered opportunities for magazines, too: a survey in the 1960s found that the relatively new habit of watching television prompted many people to read *more*, not less. One type of magazine which benefited from this was that covering leisure and pastimes, particularly the do-it-yourself market. The period saw a burgeoning of part-works, often dedicated to such topics, and the advent of consumerist magazines (*Which?* was launched in 1957). All the magazines so far discussed – representing just over a third of all magazines published in the UK – would be listed in the category of 'consumer' titles.

The tendency for such magazines, in response to changing markets, to have smaller but more closely targeted circulations during the 1960s and 1970s was paralleled in the far larger – actually, about twice as big – trade, technical and professional magazine sector. Here there was a natural tendency to smallness: the bulk of magazines in this sector had circulations measured in hundreds or at most thousands. A growing potential readership with increasing disposable incomes and more leisure time, however, proved attractive to advertisers. All the same, most titles were to say the least marginal operations, and, as well as many launches of new magazines, there were large numbers which went out of business.

Books

While it has not usually been included in narrow definitions of the media, the book publishing industry has provided employment for significant numbers of journalists. It was also subject to the same forces which impinged on the press during the 1960s and 1970s. Traditionally a small company or family firm business, publishing was characterised as being not particularly commercially-minded. As late as the 1960s paperback publishing was synonymous (at least among the public) with one publisher, Penguin Books. Many of the innovations introduced by Penguin when it was established in the 1930s – fixed price cheap books, offering value for money and sold through non-traditional outlets such as Woolworth – remained fairly novel nearly 30 years later.

At this time, publishing began to be more integrated into the conglomerate media businesses forming around press and broadcasting holdings, among them Thomson (see above) and Pearson (Longman, Penguin). The potential of the paperback mass market attracted them, and new printing technologies (described above) made publishing cheaper, more efficient, less time-consuming and more predictable. What helped with the mass production of best-selling paperbacks could also assist smaller companies to publish more specialised titles, as origination costs began to fall, reducing disadvantage of short print runs. Even in the mass market for paperbacks, a family firm like Mills and Boon could thrive. Occasionally a new small independent publisher emerged; Virago, the women's press, was one. By and large, however, the trend was towards the creation through amalgamation and take-over of large businesses with multi-media tie-ins. The numbers of small presses declined to single figures.

A media explosion?

It was possible at the end of the 1970s to talk about a media 'explosion' having occurred in the previous 15 years. It was clear that the individual media had become more closely interconnected and more transnational. Markets – readers, listeners, viewers – were changing, and in response the media had embarked on a programme of modernisation. This had called for new technologies, in particular new printing processes and improved broadcasting techniques. Web offset printing, photo-composition, computerised type-setting, colour television transmission, satellite television links, roving radio cars all made for faster, brighter communications. The volume of media output increased enormously. Nevertheless, the greatest change of all, computerisation, was not generally taken up. This suggested that the media had concentrated on reducing costs (usually through economies of scale) to sustain their traditional output – producing more for less. This made smaller-scale ventures more viable, and there were some examples of niche marketing (most notably in magazine publishing, and in the emergence of the free local newspaper). This potentially enhanced the status of journalists. There were new opportunities: the number of journalists (which had doubled in the previous 30 years) possibly increased by another 50 per cent in the decade between the late 1960s and late 1970s. Some moved into management and even media ownership. Clearly, by the beginning of the 1980s the media had gone through some quite significant changes; yet had they changed as quickly or as radically as they might? It was still commonplace to suggest that the 'revolution' had not properly begun.

7

THE MEDIA 'REVOLUTION'

> 'The danger, as always, is to
> assume that because it's there
> people will want it . . . don't
> be surprised if the media world in
> five or even ten years' time looks
> uncannily similar to today.'
>
> Steven Barnett,
> director, Media Futures programme,
> Henley Centre (1994)

The changes in the media which began to manifest themselves in the 1960s and 1970s undoubtedly accelerated in the 1980s. Media ownership became even more concentrated within transnational conglomerates, and there was more cross-media ownership. Broadcasting, and particularly television, continued to take over from the press as the dominant media form. The polarisation between the 'serious' and the 'popular' media increased, further squeezing the 'middle market'. Tabloidisation started to affect (some said infect) television. News became less important. The national commitment to public service broadcasting wavered. The ideology of Thatcherism was to encourage the gratification of the market trends which had started to show themselves in the 1970s. Government policy sought actively to promote (although it did not always secure) market competition. This further stimulated technological change, by making it more economically viable, and the most noticeable characteristic of the media in the 1980s was the wholesale shift into computer-driven technology, symbolically, as well as practically, typified by Murdoch's transfer of his newspapers to Wapping in 1986.

In the same year a local newspaper entrepreneur Eddie Shah, who ran a small weekly newspaper group in the north-west of England, launched *Today*, the first true full-colour national daily entirely produced using new technology, which allowed journalists to input their work directly into the production process. *The Independent*, a much more traditional newspaper, was launched more successfully into the 'quality' market by Andreas Whittam Smith, a former financial journalist on the *Daily Telegraph*. He was able to take advantage of the reduction in start-up costs supposedly resulting from computerisation, and the disaffection of many experienced journalists from Murdoch's *Times*. The developments of the 1980s also included, however, satellite and cable television, 'electronic books' on compact discs (CDs), and TV home shopping. What was happening in the information technology (IT) and telecommunications industries seemed to be leading to a merger of the media, IT and telecomms. Nevertheless, there was still cause to be sceptical about the power of technology.

The most significant aspects of change in the media perhaps remained those which served to satisfy changing markets, and which technology was called upon to make possible at a cost which was affordable. Newspapers such as the *Sunday Times*, which relied on advertising rather than sales for its profits, might be seen as needing to print more pages in full colour, with many specialised sections (ten or eleven in 1994) to attract more advertisers. This seemed not very much different in intention from Thomson's (admittedly more modest) decision to add a colour supplement in 1962. In television Channel 4 and breakfast television, and in radio national commercial broadcasting, appeared to satisfy similar needs for more (and more specialised) media output with, where appropriate, opportunities for advertising. Increased competition, alongside more media and changing markets, made it even more imperative for individual media to develop customer loyalty. The marketing technique of 'branding' became commonplace: even the BBC consciously branded the news. In 1994 the editor of *Campaign*, the specialist newspaper covering the advertising industry, claimed that 'the most commonly repeated mantra in the media' was that the media had to be 'treated as brands in their own right'. This included 'the medium's involvement in extra-curricular areas to strengthen its relationship with its core audience and to reach beyond that to new ones.'

Dominic Mills,
Campaign (11 March 1994)

Magazines produced tapes, CDs, books, videos and games; newspapers sold coffee cups, baseball caps, sweat suits, paper weights and table mats; and radio stations sponsored football teams, all to promote their 'image'. Perhaps the ultimate brand-building exercise (to date) was the launch in March 1994 of the *Sunday Times* credit and discount card. These efforts were often criticised for being superficial, and not dissimilar from the crude circulation building tactics last employed in the 1930s. Particularly after Robert Maxwell bought the Mirror Group in 1984 and decided to try to recover circulation lost principally to *The Sun*, Fleet Street indulged in a new round of circulation 'wars'. Papers vied with each other to give away large sums of money: even the quality press, including the *Times*, got involved in promoting games of chance often offering huge prizes.

News International appeared to introduce a more seriously competitive note when, in the summer of 1993, it unexpectedly reduced the cover price of both *The Sun* and *Times*. This flew in the face of received wisdom that newspaper prices were inelastic. Cutting cover prices would not sell more copies, it was argued, as readers were not drawn to a paper primarily on the basis of how cheap or expensive it was. Moreover, if cheaper papers did attract more readers, then they would come from other papers, and not from new readers buying for the first time. As *The Sun* and *Times* increased their circulations significantly in the following six months, News International claimed to have proved both assumptions wrong. Another indication of a new belief in the changing nature of newspapers in 'a more pluralistic, image-saturated society' came from Michael Moore, advertising director of Express Newspapers. The newspaper, he argued, was 'becoming a compendium of special interest subjects'. Some journalists talked less about publishing newspapers and more about delivering life-style statements. By the early 1990s it was more usual to refer to papers not as titles but as products. The primary concern of the media (and especially the print media) appeared to be keeping up with rapid social change.

Figure 7.1: News branding by the BBC. Advertisement in the *Guardian* (30 April 1993). Source: BBC

National newspapers

By 1994 the national newspaper industry consisted of 11 daily (five quality, three mid-market and three tabloid) and 10 Sunday (four quality, two mid-market and four tabloid) titles (see Tables 7.1 and 7.2). All these papers, except the *Financial Times*, were in a daily–Sunday partnership. Such linkages were one of the trends of the 1980s and 1990s continued from the 1960s. Only the *Daily* and *Sunday Express* connection predated 1963 unchanged. In the 1960s, the *Times* and *Sunday Times* (under Thomson), *Daily* and *Sunday Telegraph* (when the latter was launched), and *The Sun* and *News of the World* (under Murdoch) were brought together. In addition the *Sunday Pictorial* was renamed the *Sunday Mirror*, partner of the daily paper, and the *People* was bought by the Mirror Group. In 1981 Times Newspapers were sold to Murdoch; the owners of the *Daily Mail* launched the *Mail on Sunday* the following year; *The Independent* produced a Sunday version in 1990; and the *Guardian* took over the *Observer* in 1993.

This represented two prominent trends. First, newspaper owners again shuffled the pack: half the national dailies and eight national Sundays changed hands. Second, the concentration of ownership increased. The two daily and two Sunday newspapers successfully launched after 1980 were all owned by conglomerates by 1994. In fact, the four largest groups produced almost 90 per cent of the national daily and Sunday newspapers sold. Murdoch's News International (*The Sun, News of the World, Times, Sunday Times, Today*) had just over a 34 per cent share; the Mirror Group (*Daily* and *Sunday Mirror, Daily Record, People, Independent, Independent on Sunday*) nearly 30 per cent; United Newspapers (*Daily* and *Sunday Express, Daily Star*) more than 13 per cent; and the Associated Newspapers (*Daily Mail* and *Mail on Sunday*) nearly 13 per cent. The two next largest owners, the Hollinger Group (*Daily* and *Sunday Telegraph*) and the Guardian Media Group (which included the *Observer*) together accounted for another 8.5 per cent. In sum, then, six groups owned the entire national press, except the *Financial Times* and *Sunday Sport*. This concentration alarmed many, including the European Commission which investigated the phenomenon in 1992, and noted that the United Kingdom alone had no clear constitutional guarantee of public access to the media.

These changes in ownership coincided with a change in style: before the relaunch of *The Sun* in 1969 there were only two tabloid newspapers

Table 7.1: National daily newspaper circulations (millions)

Newspaper	1985	1994 (Nov)	%
Daily Telegraph	1.202	1.071	
Times	0.478	0.606	
Financial Times	0.234	0.293	
Guardian	0.487	0.404	
Independent	—	0.290	
Total quality	**2.401**	**2.664**	**+10.9**
Daily Express	1.902	1.303	
Daily Mail	1.815	1.739	
Today	—	0.583	
Total middle	**3.717**	**3.625**	**−2.5**
Daily Mirror	3.033	2.481	
Sun	4.125	4.053	
Daily Star	1.455	0.743	
Total tabloid	**8.613**	**7.277**	**−15.5**
Total market	**14.731**	**13.566**	**−7.9**

Sources: ABC; Colin-Seymour-Ure, *The British Press and Broadcasting since 1945* (Oxford, 1991)

which survived the 1970s, the *Daily* and *Sunday Mirror*. In the following 20 years a further nine newspapers either converted to tabloid format or were launched as tabloids. (Another three launched as tabloids but failed to survive beyond 1988.) By the 1990s there was not a single broadsheet middle-market or 'popular' newspaper. As we have seen, the national newspaper industry was in long-term decline. Total circulations fell steadily over 35 years until by 1994 they were only two-thirds of what they had been in 1957. The Sunday papers lost nearly half their readers in the same period.

Ironically, new technology was supposed to launch a new 'golden age' for the national press. The number of national papers in circulation rose by four (*Independent, Independent on Sunday, Today* and *Sunday Sport*)

Table 7.2: National Sunday newspaper circulations (millions)

Newspaper	1985	1994 (Nov)	%
Observer	0.736	0.510	
Sunday Times	1.251	1.302	
Sunday Telegraph	0.686	0.669	
Independent on Sunday	—	0.315	
Total quality	**2.673**	**2.796**	+ 4.6
Sunday Express	2.449	1.430	
Mail on Sunday	1.631	1.942	
Total middle	**4.080**	**3.372**	−17.3
News of the World	5.103	4.775	
People	2.962	2.032	
Sunday Mirror	3.009	2.513	
Sunday Sport	—	0.323	
Total tabloid	**11.074**	**9.643**	−12.9
Total market	**17.827**	**15.811**	−11.56

Sources: ABC; Colin-Seymour-Ure, *The British Press and Broadcasting since 1945* (Oxford, 1991)

between 1985 and 1994. Four others which launched (*Sunday Today, News on Sunday, The Post* and *Sunday Correspondent*) rapidly folded. This expansion in the number of titles, taken together, probably added at best no more than 200,000 to the total number of national daily newspapers sold, and less than 300,000 to national Sunday circulations. Immediately after the turning-point year of 1986, there was a brief resurgence. Total circulations rose marginally by about 2 per cent to a new high in 1988. In the longer run, however, they fell by 2.9m, or 9 per cent, between 1985 (32.56m) and 1994 (29.66m). Factors proposed for the decline included the rising relative cost of buying a paper (by 1994 the *Sunday Times* cost £1); more television output carrying more advertising, some of it taken from the press; the economic recession of the late 1980s which resulted in general reductions in levels of advertising; and a failure to replace older readers with young ones. These probably further emphasised the benefits of concentration with its cross-media promotion opportunities, revenue generation and economies of scale. By 1994 none of the four newspapers launched after 1986 remained in independent ownership. The *Daily Star* was in any event the product of a large group (Express Newspapers); but *Today*, which was seen originally as breaking the mould of Fleet Street, was swallowed up by the biggest conglomerate, News International, and eventually moved to Wapping. What was arguably the most ambitious venture of all, *The Independent*, which was started by a consortium of journalists who raised financial backing in the City, was taken over (along with the Sunday paper started in 1990) by the Mirror Group in 1994.

Provincial press

In 1994 the provincial press was made up of 16 morning, 73 evening, 10 Sunday, 820 paid for weekly and about 1,000 free newspapers. (The figures are necessarily imprecise as definitions of what constitutes a title differ. These figures include all separate editions.) Mostly the sector had been in steady decline over the previous 15 years. The most obvious change during that period was among the weekly papers: about half of the traditional paid for titles disappeared, while the number of free-sheets rose to a peak of 1,156 in 1990. Free-sheets outnumbered the paid for titles from 1987. If counting titles was not wholly reliable, circulation figures told the story.

Paid for weekly newspaper circulations fell over 15 years on average by 50 per cent, and total sales from 9.7 million in 1981 to 7.7 million in 1993. By comparison in 1991 a total of 43.5 million free-sheets were circulated (although the figure had fallen to 32.9 million by 1993). The major impact of the free-sheets came in the early 1980s: circulations virtually doubled from 15.3 million to 29.9 million between 1981 and 1983. In the ten years up to 1985 the free-sheets' share of total provincial newspaper advertising revenues quadrupled from 6.4 per cent to 26.2 per cent: by 1990 it was 35 per cent. At the same time, the morning and evening papers also struggled: their combined circulations fell from 7.1 million in 1981 to 5.6 million in 1993. The evening papers, and particularly those in major cities, were harder hit (see Table 7.3).

On average their circulations fell 25 per cent (around a third in the big conurbations) over 15 years.

Table 7.3: Selected regional morning and evening newspaper circulations (thousands)

Newspaper	1987/8	1994 (Jan–Jun)	%
Mornings			
Birmingham Post	25	27.5	+ 10
Western Daily Press	74	65.2	−11.9
Northern Echo	88	80.5	− 8.5
Yorkshire Post	92	81.6	−11.3
Daily Post (Liverpool)	70	74.9	+ 7
Western Mail	77	68.6	−10.9
(Glasgow) Herald	123	113.3	− 7.9
Scotsman	86	83.6	− 2.8
Evenings			
Birmingham Evening Mail	233	200.5	−13.9
Telegraph and Argus (Bradford)	81	63.2	−22
Grimsby Evening Telegraph	73	48.8	−33.1
Evening Star (Ipswich)	36	30.1	−16.4
Leicester Mercury	146	122	−16.4
Manchester Evening News	291	214	−26.5
Northampton Chronicle & Echo	39	30.7	−21.3
Belfast Telegraph	148	136.7	− 7.6

Sources: ABC; Colin-Seymour-Ure, *The British Press and Broadcasting since 1945* (Oxford, 1991)

Evening newspaper circulations totalled 4.2m in 1993, a decline of 17 per cent in only five years. (Circulations of the morning papers fell on average 17 per cent over 15 years.) The performance of the small number of provincial Sunday newspapers (10 in 1994) ran against this trend. There were several launches – *Wales on Sunday, Sunday Life,*

Scotland on Sunday (all Thomson papers), *Yorkshire on Sunday*, and a Northern edition of *Sunday World* (Dublin), although the *Sunday News* (Belfast) closed. The Sunday papers had total circulations of 2.57m in 1993 (1.34m in 1975). The London evenings, however, reflected the general trend. In 1975 the market had been for 1.13m copies: by 1994 the sole survivor, the *Evening Standard* was selling about 460,000. (The *Daily Record* was a special case as for most of the 1980s its circulation of about 750,000 was included in that of the *Daily Mirror*.) Throughout the 1980s and into 1990s the question regularly asked was, why did so many people no longer want to buy a local paper?

Two sets of factors – one economic, the other social – were proposed. Unemployment, recession and general economic decline were seen not only as discouraging people from buying papers whose cover prices had actually risen about twice as fast as inflation, but as making them less interested in the goods and services advertised in those papers. The Henley Centre found that as the cover price of a weekly paper in an urban area rose, sales fell; and as affluence rose, so did circulation – all in more or less the same proportions. Urban depopulation also had an effect. By far the biggest impact, however, came from social factors. During the 1980s the extent to which people relied primarily on television for news, rather than newspapers, doubled. Changing work patterns, including more working women and in many places fewer working men; a declining inclination to read (allied perhaps to falling literacy standards), and competition for leisure time were also important. The Henley research found that in sum social factors accounted for nearly half the total decline in the sales of weekly papers over a ten-year period. That was actually greater than the impact of free-sheets.

Yet for the most part provincial newspapers remained profitable, if often only marginally so. The reason was that the rationalisation begun in the 1960s was continued. New technology was widely introduced. The larger newspapers – and groups – led the way, as switching to electronic systems was seen as one way of securing economies of scale. By the beginning of the 1990s some papers were introducing third-generation systems and paperless news rooms. The adoption of new technology was largely dependent on the economic benefits it was likely to deliver and the availability of the capital to pay for it. It went hand-in-hand with further concentration of ownership, and the new free-sheets, which were largely the products of independent entrepreneurs, were not immune. By 1987 two-thirds of free-sheets were owned by groups. In 1989, of the eight largest owners of free titles, seven were also major paid for newspaper groups. Together they accounted for nearly 45 per cent of the free-sheet market. The same seven – Thomson, Reed, Northcliffe, United, Westminster, EMAP and The Guardian – also controlled 52 per cent of paid for newspaper circulations. Further exchanges of titles in the 1990s ensured greater geographical concentration of interests. Thomson, EMAP and Reed were all active in both buying and selling from each other and acquiring newspapers from other owners. By 1991 more than 80 per cent of the local press was controlled by 15 corporations; more than 60 per cent by ten – all of them cross-media owners. In some geographical areas individual companies controlled more than 75 per cent of the local newspaper circulations. Nevertheless, cost-cutting was deemed essential.

By the end of the 1980s the paid weekly newspapers' share of national advertising had fallen in 20 years by more than 40 per cent and the daily papers' share by 37 per cent. The economic downturn which began in the late 1980s added to the problems. Provincial newspapers had relied on job advertising for as much as a third of their ad revenue: in some cases, such advertising fell by 50 per cent at the beginning of the 1990s. Newspapers made attempts to generate new sources of advertising, but the main effort went into making savings. Computerisation led to severe reductions in (sometimes the elimination of) production staff such as compositors. A number of large groups reduced their workforces by hundreds virtually overnight. Journalists were affected, too, however. Researchers at the University of Central Lancashire found examples of a newspaper circulating more than 100,000 copies a week with only six journalists; a paper where the number of journalists had been cut from 12 to six in five years; and a centralised production centre where 12 sub-editors produced material for 24 titles. Elsewhere, a group claimed to have cut its editorial staff by 50 per cent.

8

THE MEDIA 'REVOLUTION': 2

Television

Changes in television in the 1980s and 1990s more than matched those in newspapers. The period saw the introduction of satellite broadcasting; a fourth terrestrial channel; breakfast television, and the reshaping of ITV. (The cable 'revolution' which had been promised failed to materialise.) By 1993 dozens of television channels were available where 11 years previously there had been only three. The whole nature of British television was altered. Satellite television remained to some extent beyond the State regulation which had characterised broadcasting virtually since its inception. The merger of the two original broadcasters into BSkyB, half owned by Murdoch, questioned the whole British approach to television. If BSkyB had been a terrestrial broadcaster, Murdoch would not have been allowed so large a stake in it alongside his ownership of the News International newspapers. The government's response, however, was not to apply the existing regulations covering terrestrial broadcasting, but to develop a policy which favoured the 'open market' in television espoused by Murdoch. The auctioning of ITV franchises was introduced under the 1990 Broadcasting Act. This resulted in four companies (notably TV-am and Thames) losing their franchises. In some instances where there was competition for franchises, the levels of the winning bids put additional pressure on the franchisees to make ITV profitable. In 1994 restrictions on the cross-ownership of the 16 independent television companies were eased. These were the manifestations of a government policy founded on the belief that the intrusion of market forces would result in the emergence of broadcasting organisations of enterprise and financial strength. The argument was that in an increasingly competitive global market, American and other European media conglomerates were increasing in both size and power. The British presence in the world market had been effectively restricted to the BBC. If British television were not strong enough, it would itself be taken over by predatory foreign companies. A number of companies merged, or were involved in takeovers. Carlton and Granada, two of the biggest ITV companies, gained control of Central and LWT respectively: there was a merger between Anglia and Meridian. Existing cross-ownership (Central had shares in Meridian) complicated matters.

There were few (but powerful) vocal supporters of government policy. Even those who favoured the formation of media conglomerates complained about the retention of regulations preventing the large press companies, such as Reed and Associated Newspapers, from owning more than a minority share in ITV companies. They restricted the growth of individual media organisations. Under the regulations no British company would become large enough to compete globally. Others argued that the piecemeal approach adopted resulted in one organisation (Carlton–Central) owning 30 per cent of ITV while no one else was permitted to acquire more than 23 per cent. Greg Dyke, who resigned from LWT after it was taken over by Granada, argued that the cross-ownership rules were 'ridiculously parochial in a context of global information and entertainment, global media players'.

* 'If News International can own five national papers and as many satellite channels as it wants, it makes no sense to restrict everyone else.'

Guardian (14 March 1994)

The more commonly expressed fear, however, was that the emergence of large television companies would 'signal the death-knell of the already creaking federal structure of ITV – and with it an era of British programme-making' (Will Hutton; *Guardian*, 7 December 1993). The greatest pressure was seen as coming in the areas of news and current affairs and documentary-making. The Broadcasting Act established the network centre to control the shared programming across ITV. This, too, represented a move towards greater commercialism, as the centre's predecessor body, the ITV Association, had been a purely administrative organisation. One immediate fear was the current affairs and documentary programmes would be subjected to new tests of commercial viability. Programmes that did not attract large audiences would be dropped.

One of the major current affairs programmes previously shown across the network, This Week, disappeared when its producer, Thames, lost its franchise. Although the Broadcasting Act included a 'quality threshold', it was felt that the network centre would replace This Week with less investigative programming. Also considered to be at risk was Granada's World in Action. Such fears were exacerbated when, at the first strategy conference of the 15 regional franchise holders organised by the network centre in June 1993, it was suggested that ITN's News at Ten be moved to an early evening slot. The proposal resulted in uproar with Dyke, chairman of the ITV council, called to give evidence before the National Heritage committee. In the spring of 1994, World in Action was eventually suspended in the middle of a series to make way for ITV's response (initially a double episode of Coronation Street and a James Bond film) to a BBC decision to run an additional Monday evening episode of EastEnders.

All these changes in commercial television had their effects on the BBC. The Corporation admitted that with the introduction of satellite television it was inevitable that it would lose overall market share. This raised fundamental questions about the licence fee. Could the BBC properly levy a charge on the entire television-owning population when it commanded perhaps less than a third of the total audience? Although the amount of time people spent watching television altered little, by 1992 the BBC's share of the total terrestrial audience had fallen from 50 per cent to 42.7 per cent. The Corporation's response to the changes across television came to be represented by the approach of its director general John Birt. 'Birtism' consisted of a more enterprising managerialism alongside a commitment to programming of what Birt called in 1993 'high ambition'. In news and current affairs Birt claimed that the BBC had 'a mission to explain'. This was translated as an attempt to move the BBC up-market and away from 'tabloid TV'. Many journalists publicly supported Birtism, while others found the managerial style disruptive and demoralising.

With the BBC's charter due for renewal by the government in 1996, Birtism was an attempt to identify a new role for the Corporation into the twenty-first century. In the 1980s the BBC had come under increasing attack from the Conservative government for its supposed financial irresponsibility and political bias. As part of the general change in television, which also affected ITV, the Corporation had to move towards offering a quarter of its programming to independent producers. It began to look increasingly unlikely that the BBC could survive the 1990s intact as the institution built by Lord Reith before and immediately after World War II. The foundation of this edifice was Reith's dictum that the BBC's role was to educate, inform and entertain. As the charter renewal date came closer there were fears that the pressures to entertain would outstrip the dedication to educate and inform. There was also enthusiasm, however, that, while Birt made considerable managerial changes, he would strengthen the BBC's journalism.

What neither the BBC nor the independent companies appeared to be able to do much about was the steady decline in audiences for news and current affairs. Research indicated that television remained the main source of news for the overwhelming majority of people: about 80 per cent relied on television, compared to about 25 per cent who preferred a national newspaper. (The figures were different for local news: about 30 per cent television and about 60 per cent local paper.) Most people (about 70 per cent) also trusted television news to be unbiased: only 8 per cent trusted newspapers. Researchers claimed that such figures were a more reliable measure of the audiences for news than crude viewing figures. They indicated the extent to which people found television news satisfying rather than how many people simply had their sets turned on. Steven Barnett, of the Henley Centre, argued in 1989 that television news audiences were much like newspaper readers. That suggested that there was an audience for both middle-market and 'tabloid' television news. Sky News on satellite television claimed to be 'a little more *Daily Mail* than anything else', and News at Ten was widely criticised for moving down-market. The advent of The Big Breakfast on Channel 4, with virtually no news content, excited most fears that the Reithian model was being abandoned. Barnett raised the prospect of 'glamourising pressures' resulting in 'an insidious trivialisation process which would . . . undermine professional journalistic values . . .' (*British Journalism Review*, 1989).

Radio

Many of the structural changes in television were felt in radio, too. The independent sector expanded, particularly into areas previously monopolised by the BBC, and the Corporation developed a strategy in response which was clearly Birtist. By 1993 nearly 90 per cent of the adult population listened to radio. Traditionally, by far the major part of that audience had been tuned to the BBC. The most popular station was Radio 1 which reached more than a third of all adults. A shifting emphasis was evident, however. By 1993 the BBC had 39 regional stations with 10.4 million listeners. There were more than 140 ILR stations with 21 million listeners. The following year represented something of a watershed for commercial radio. For the first time, its total audience (27.7 million) exceeded that of the BBC (27.6 million). Overall, radio was one of the major media growth areas. Not only did the number of hours people spent listening rise sharply, but the medium's share of advertising doubled from two per cent (where it had been for decades) to four per cent, with forecasts that it would grow to five per cent by 1997. This expansion was largely the result of the Conservative government's commitment to 'extending choice' and encouraging the growth of the commercial sector. The BBC's monopoly of national broadcasting was ended in 1992. Together, the independent broadcasters began to reduce the BBC's share of the radio audience by significant amounts. In response, the BBC embarked on a series of changes of its own.

There was a plan to move Radio 4 exclusively to FM. This was dropped after national protests. In 1993 Radio 1 underwent something of a transformation when a number of the on-air personnel were dropped. The Corporation's most obvious move was to launch Radio 5, then relaunch it in 1994 as Radio 5 Live. The first two national independent radio ventures, Classic FM and Virgin 1215, were essentially music stations (although Classic emphasised its news output). Similarly, few ILR stations carried much news. Their major impact was on Radios 1 and 2. Many of the new, as well as the expansionist, proprietors in commercial radio, such as Virgin and Chrysalis, had their roots in the music industry. The national non-music station Talk Radio UK, which began broadcasting early in 1995, was seen as a direct threat, however, to Radios 4 and 5 Live. From the beginning Radio 5 was to a large extent news and sport oriented: it was estimated that for its launch the BBC recruited up to 160 journalists. Its successor,

Radio 5 Live was even more news driven. It probably created an additional 80 jobs for journalists. One possible problem with the formula was its tendency to alienate women listeners. Radio 5 Live also enjoyed an uneasy relationship with Radio 4, which was still widely regarded as the BBC's flagship news and current affairs station. By 1995 there was considerable uncertainty over the future of radio journalism – ironically at precisely the time when the medium was at its most popular.

Magazines

In 1994 there were approximately 7,000 magazines and periodicals being published in the United Kingdom (about 2,500 consumer titles and 4,500 trade magazines). In the decade after 1984 the total number grew by 73 per cent. Magazines in general were highly dependent on advertising (many titles were given away), and in the 1980s it was predicted that there would be significant, perhaps even fatal, losses of revenue to television and radio. This declining share of ad revenues (down to 14 per cent of all media spending in 1992) was reflected in structural changes in the sector. The most obvious and important of these was the launch of several consumer titles, particularly those aimed at women. Moreover, about half of them were trans-European ventures. This, too, was a significant diversion from previous practice.

The first forays were made by continental European publishers to the United Kingdom. The German companies Gruner and Jahr and Bauer launched *Prima* and *Best*, and *Bella* respectively in 1987. They were followed by the Spanish weekly *Hello!*. Subsequently, News International and IPC entered into arrangements with French publishers to launch *Elle* and *Marie Claire* in the United Kingdom (both 1988). Eventually, there was a British export to continental Europe, the IPC title *Essentials*. More than in newspapers or (so far) broadcasting the consumer magazine business became a trans-European industry, with editorial, management and printing offices spread across the continent. This has been compared to the internationalisation of motor car manufacturing in which parts are both made and assembled in plants in different countries. The most obvious reason behind this Europeanisation of consumer magazines was the cost savings arising from economies of scale. By the mid-1980s, however, the number of women reading a magazine was less than half what it had been 30 years previously, it was estimated. The new titles revived the market. In addition, distribution changed to allow newsagents to return unsold copies, which led to more titles being displayed. This was also thought to have stimulated sales.

In all, about a dozen new major weekly and monthly women's titles appeared between 1985 and 1990. Their impact on existing magazines was huge (see Tables 8.1 and 8.2). In the ten years after 1982 each of the established women's weekly titles lost on average more than 40 per cent of their readers, and the monthlies about 20 per cent. The circulations of *Woman's Own* and *Woman* fell by a third in five years. By 1992 the two biggest selling women's titles were *Bella* and another Bauer magazine, *Take a Break* (1990). Despite the success of these individual titles, continental European publishers remained a relatively small part of the UK industry. IPC (Reed International) was still the biggest publisher of both consumer and trade magazines. In 1992 the company consolidated that position by merging with the Dutch publisher Elsevier. Thereafter Reed–Elsevier embarked on a major programme of acquisitions buying at least 25 other companies. At about the same time EMAP bought a series of titles previously owned by Robert Maxwell, and Thomson Information Services. This made EMAP the second largest publisher of trade magazines in the United Kingdom.

Table 8.1: Selected women's weekly magazine circulations (in thousands)

Title	1982	1993	%
Best (1987)		563	
Chat (1985)		480	
Hello (1988)		472	
Me (1989)		359	
My Weekly	832	428	−49
People's Friend	690	477	−31
Woman	1,456	742	−49
Woman's Own	1,551	729	−53
Woman's Realm	747	368	−51
Woman's Weekly	1,483	796	−46

Sources: Janice Winship, *Inside Women's Magazines* (London, 1987); ABC

Table 8.2: Selected women's monthly magazine circulations (in thousands)

Title	1984	1993 (July–Dec)	%
Company	212	261	+23
Cosmopolitan	387	457	+18
Elle (1985)		221	
Essentials (1988)		380	
Family Circle	543	340	−37
Good Housekeeping	353	468	+33
Living	423	161	−62
Marie Claire (1988)		368	
Prima (1986)		613	
She	221	252	+14
Vogue	137	179	+31
Woman and Home	600	435	−28

Sources: Janice Winship, *Inside Women's Magazines* (London, 1987); ABC

Books

The conglomeration, transnationalism and concentration of ownership apparent in the magazine industry in the 1980s and 1990s had a parallel in book publishing. Most obviously, Murdoch emerged as a major owner of publishing houses, including HarperCollins. Independent firms, such as Virago, were swallowed up by corporations. The traditional, small publishing house was generally mourned, as famous imprints were apparently turned into corporate brands. Publishing succumbed to the marketing ethos, and titles were sold literally off supermarket shelves. The number of titles increased enormously: in 1993 80,000 were published. Volume sales were the key to success in mainstream publishing. Technological advances which linked authors to printers *via* the publisher reduced costs. More importantly this computerisation increased flexibility. The production process no longer took months: a book could move from typescript to finished bound copy in days. This meant that the importance of estimating likely sales (always a matter of guesswork) was reduced. Reprinting became a viable option. Yet it was this flexibility which also permitted the re-emergence of smaller, independent publishers.

A number of such companies were founded in the 1980s, among them Bloomsbury, The Women's Press, Fourth Estate and Headline. It became possible to edit and produce books with small staffs using computers, and to print short runs, sometimes only hundreds of copies. After 1988 the number of small independent presses increased quite dramatically. By 1993 there were estimated to be several hundred trading successfully. Many professed to adhere to traditional publishing values. The big conglomerates 'just see £ signs,' Joanna Prior, the marketing director of Fourth Estate said in 1994. All the same, there was no reason why an independent had to stay small. In 1993 Headline acquired the traditional publisher, Hodder and Stoughton.

In 1994 the Campaign for Press and Broadcasting Freedom produced a diagram charting media ownership in the United Kingdom. While the web of shared interests was complex, the overall pattern was reasonably clear: the majority of significant media owners had large shares in several media, forming more or less powerful media groups most of which overlapped with each other. For example, Carlton Television, as well as owning Central TV, had shares in ITN (which also owned the former Independent Radio News), GMTV and the London News Network (LNN). Carlton's shareholding partners in ITN included Reuters, Granada Television and Anglia Television; in LNN London Weekend Television (LWT), and in GMTV the Guardian Media Group (GMG). LWT was owned by Granada. Reuters also operated its own television news service, supplying (among others) GMTV, as well as its better known wire service, subscribed to by Guardian Media Group newspapers. GMG's interests included Anglia Television. Central had shares in Meridian which was controlled by MAI which owned Anglia.

The tendency to crossmedia conglomeration seemed unstoppable. In May 1994 the BBC and Pearson, owner of the *Financial Times*, Penguin Books, Thames Television and Westminster Press, announced a joint world-wide venture. This only provoked speculation that Murdoch's News Corporation was planning a link-up with the Italian media owner Silvio Berlusconi. In global terms, the concentration of media interests in Britain was relatively small-scale. The BBC–Pearson agreement involved an initial investment of £30m. In October 1993 Tele-Communications and Bell Atlantic effected a $33 billion merger, the biggest in American history. Nevertheless, government policy hinged on British corporations being able to stake a claim in the world media market.

Media regulation was seen as either undesirable or impossible as communications proliferated. In newspapers, broadcasting, magazines and books production became increasingly cost led. This threatened the pluralistic approach, embodied in broadcasting, and which had been characteristic of the British media for nearly a century. The new objective was to maximise audiences, leading, it was felt by many, to the 'tabloidisation' of the media. The counter was Murdoch's assertion that, as the technology advanced both to reduce costs and to facilitate access, anyone could get into the media. Experience showed, however, that those opportunities remained rare in the 1980s and 1990s. An independent sector flourished only in book publishing and, to a lesser extent, in magazines. The question was whether this was compatible with journalistic notions of freedom of expression.

9

NEWS

'Journalists shelter under a monumental
delusion. They believe the news they write
about affects the lives of the general public
and that there is some obligation upon
newspapers to report, in depth, the grave
issues and conflicts which beset the world.
There is no such influence and no such obligation
because that is not what people buy newspapers *for*.'

Tom Gallacher

'. . . there were a number of "newspaper"
films showing at the local cinema in which
reporters would rush into the news-room
at the last minute, yelling,
"Hold the front page!" . . . It wasn't long
before my ambitions were clearly defined:
I wanted to become a *great* press photographer
and I wanted to work for a *great* newspaper . . .'

Terry Fincher
The Terry Fincher File (London, 1981)

Journalists, as Denis McQuail found when he prepared a working paper for the Royal Commission on the Press (1974–77), believe they 'know news when they see it'. They also recognise its importance. Mark Damazer, editor of the BBC's television news programmes, said in 1994, 'News is very central to what the BBC does.' In the same week Martin Lindsay, editor of the *Sunday Life* in Belfast, which was voted the best daily or Sunday provincial newspaper of 1993, said bluntly: 'News sells newspapers.' One authority has gone as far as saying that news is 'pure journalism', and news has been at the core of journalism training. Yet the very fact that it has been necessary to defend news in this way indicates the extent to which journalists have themselves become unsure about news, and its role. Facing up to the long-term decline in consumption of news, one provincial newspaper editor argued

> '. . . journalists must recognise that their futures lie in marketing useful information rather than writing news stories.'
> *The Changing Vision* (Preston, 1993)

The question, 'What is news?' has been a standard one asked of all journalists at the outset of their careers. There has never seemed to be a satisfactory answer. This has been a reflection of the notion that news itself has not generally been seen as presenting many problems, while on the other hand, the *way* in which the news is reported has. Yet news *is* reports; according to the *Oxford English Dictionary*,

> 'the report or account of recent occurrences brought or coming to one as new information; new occurrences as a subject of report or talk.'

The use of the word 'news' directly to describe new things in themselves properly became obsolete centuries ago. A verb 'to news', meaning to report, was in use up to the beginning of the twentieth century. So, strictly speaking, news has not been simply 'out there', happening. Nevertheless, the popular idea has arisen that news was events. The term 'the news' became detached from reports, even though (or perhaps because) the press and broadcasting became increasingly competent in presenting news. The phrase 'to tell someone the news' (to inform them) implied that 'the news' was somehow separate from the telling.

Attempts to define 'news' in its modern form tended only to complicate matters. When Harold Evans, a former editor of the *Times* and *Sunday Times*, said 'News is people', he seemed to be substituting one category for another. What Evans almost certainly meant was that reports needed to be what people wanted to read, which in the age of the 'human interest' story was mostly about other people. Events (and people) could be seen as the raw materials of 'news'. A definition of news produced in the 1970s said it was 'a product manufactured from what is available'. So, Arthur McEwan, the editor of the *San Francisco Examiner*, who said 'news is whatever a good editor chooses to print' was close to the mark. That has begged another set of questions about *how* editorial choices are made. It has also placed the journalist – and neither events nor people – at the centre of the news-making process. Journalists have made news. One way in which they have done so has been by elevating it to an art form. News values, *UK Press Gazette* observed in 1992, were

> 'acquired like some masonic faith, inculcated into the journalist over years and passed down through an oral tradition which has accepted little change in direction or belief. We all know what makes a story, don't we?'

By the 1990s that question could no longer be confidently answered in the affirmative.

As recently as 1985, Alastair Hetherington, a former editor of the *Guardian*, declared, after studying both academic analyses and journalistic practices, that news values depended on two criteria:

> (1) what is the political, social, economic and human *importance* of the event? And (2) will it *interest*, excite and entertain our audience? *The first takes precedence over the second . . .*'
> *News, Newspaper and Television*
> (London, 1985) – my emphasis

Even Kelvin MacKenzie, editor of *The Sun*, which was held by many to have been responsible for the decline of 'real' journalism, argued

> '*The Sun* believes that a newspaper's first duty is to publish the news . . . By the time [the millions who read *The Sun*] put down their paper at the end of the day, there are very few political, social or economic stories they do not know about.'
> *UK Press Gazette* (1987)

In a week *The Sun* carried more 'real, *bona fide*, hard stories . . . political, economic, home and international', according to Andrew Knight, than *The Independent* and almost as many as the *Times*. That seemed difficult to reconcile with the paper's reputation. *The Sun*'s extraordinary success in the 1970s and 1980s was often seen as having been founded on the highly effective non-news formula; pandering to the prejudices of the readers, as one former tabloid journalist called it.

An earlier Royal Commission on the Press (1947–49) found when it surveyed journalists, newspaper owners and managers, that was precisely what the papers did. The interests of the average audience were deemed to be, first, sport followed by 'news about people . . . whose sentiment or excitement brings some colour into life'. What readers were thought not to have much interest in was 'public affairs'. By the mid-1970s the situation seemed to have changed quite dramatically, although a Royal Commission minority report castigated 'the vacuity and irresponsibility of some of our popular newspapers'. Hetherington was in no doubt in 1985: 'Public affairs,' he wrote, 'are now at the top of the list, instead of the bottom, even in some, though not all, of the popular papers'.

That conclusion seemed to fly in the face of experience. *The Sun*'s success, the former *Evening Standard* editor Charles Wintour pointed out, was founded not on news but on 'Plenty of competitions, naked breasts, free offers, excellent sports coverage and endless exploitation of sex stories . . .'. Many provincial newspapers, which were under severe economic pressure (see Chapter 7), tried to emulate *The Sun*, and a study identified 'a long-term tendency . . . towards entertainment trivia and sensationalism based on the lowest common denominator'. What was 'important' often clashed with what was 'interesting'.

What is news?

What most journalists have agreed on is that there are no absolute news values. They have arisen out of a coming together of commercial interest (media ownership), professionalism (journalism), and consumption (audiences) in deciding on the significance ('importance') and 'interest' of events. Any (or all) of these elements are variable, and are likely to be affected by a number of additional factors, including timing; size; closeness (physical and cultural); familiarity (or surprise); relevance; personalities; power, and availability. Academic analysts have sought to construct the 'ideal' news story from these building blocks. One much-quoted attempt in the 1960s produced this model:

> a big event, which was easily understood, clearly relevant to the audience, and not too out of the ordinary (unless it was totally unexpected), occurring in one of the major nations, preferably involving somebody already well known, who could be photographed, and happening in time to make the media's deadlines. If

it were a negative story, so much the better, largely because that made any event stand out and appear unambiguous.

It appeared that certain categories of stories fitted the model better than others: domestic political scandals, natural disasters, wars and revolutions (depending on where they occurred), major accidents. News was a formula.

Journalists have sought to refute this. They have emphasised their own professional contribution to the news process, usually expressed in three ways. (1) They claimed to make sense of what John Whale, a former *Sunday Times* journalist, called 'random events' in a largely unknown world by giving them recognisable shape. (2) They revealed the hidden, the secret and the corrupt 'in the public interest'. This has been encapsulated in a (probably apocryphal) saying attributed to both Hearst and Harmsworth that 'News is something that somebody somewhere doesn't want you to print. All the rest is advertising.' (3) Finally, they have claimed an importance for journalistic 'flair', 'style', and editorial direction. Mike Molloy, a former editor of the *Daily Mirror*, has asserted that an editor

> 'must instinctively know the man and woman out there, what they love, hate, dream about, are indifferent to, the prejudices they cherish and the passions he must now articulate. It is not a mystical state. I have seen the process repeated successfully throughout my life.'
>
> *Guardian* (April 1990)

The price of failure was dismissal (for editors), bankruptcy (for proprietors), or closure (for individual papers). By the 1990s, however, journalism as a whole appeared to be confronting failure. It seemed either to be out of touch with (and losing) its audiences, or, where it succeeded in attracting readers and viewers, to be abandoning its traditional values. The *British Journalism Review* argued in its inaugural issue in 1989 that 'poisonous weeds . . . [were] choking the life-blood out of British journalism', and complained about 'a contagious outbreak of squalid, banal, lazy and cowardly journalism whose only qualification is that it helps to make newspaper publishers (and some journalists) rich'.

While proprietors such as Beaverbrook and Thomson remained primarily interested in propaganda or making money from advertising, and broadcasting was closely regulated, journalists had considerable power over deciding the news agenda. Above all, news was 'important'. Of the values discussed above, power, size, familiarity and proximity were paramount. Journalists saw themselves as intermediaries between 'important' events and people, and their audiences. Journalists largely determined what was relevant, and even the relative value of personalities. Proprietors were not powerless and audiences were considered. (The *Daily Herald* was a TUC paper, and the *Daily Mirror* claimed with some justification in the 1940s and 1950s to be the voice of the working-class.) Journalists, however, believed they either shared, or articulated the views of their audiences. Under this regime, news was primarily

> 'Fires, explosions, floods, . . . railway accidents, destructive storms, earthquakes, shipwrecks . . . accidents . . . street riots . . . strikes . . . the suicide of persons of note, social or political, and murders of a sensational or atrocious character.'

This list could have described most of the contents of a national daily newspaper as recently as the 1960s, television news into the 1970s and the local press in the 1980s. Some papers and bulletins were still carrying a predominance of such news in the 1990s. A writer in *UK Press Gazette* observed in 1990 that the list 'remains as good an indication of what constitutes news today as when it was first issued'. That was for Reuters' correspondents in 1883.

This gave news a particular set of characteristics. First, it tended to be reactive: events happened, and then they were reported. Second, the bigger the event (or the more important the personality), the bigger the story. Third, there was a premium on being the first to reveal a particular event: journalists hunted 'scoops'. Fourth, a story was no good if it was not ready when the paper printed, or the news was broadcast: news was to a large extent determined by timing. Finally, news in the United Kingdom was extremely parochial (literally in some instances), as journalists instinctively interpreted what was important to their audiences as being 'close to home'. In television this was sometimes known as McLurg's Law, and the former editor of the *Daily Mail*, Bill Hardcastle, came up with an elaborate formula to explain it. In short, the further away from your own doorstep an event, the less important it was. This also presumed that most news arose from familiar circumstances, in particular the daily, weekly, monthly, annual round of established events. Newspapers and bulletins concentrated on what was called 'hard' news (what constituted 'hard' news is in the Reuters list above). There was, of course, 'soft' news which, as well as the human interest story, became a mainstay of 'popular' journalism. The agenda for this, however, did not vary greatly from that of 'hard' news. What was carried was essentially news about the United Kingdom, British people and British interests, represented primarily by the Establishment. (The principles, adjusted for special interests, applied equally to publications such as the *Financial Times, Jewish Chronicle* and *Woman's Realm.*)

The emphases in the 'popular' and 'serious' press (broadcasting tended to be 'serious') differed, especially in tone and the prominence given to individual stories, but the content remained essentially the same. This applied to the provincial press as much as to national newspapers. 'Real' news was obvious, and it helped determine where journalists looked for stories. Sources were to be found in parliament, local government, the political parties, the civil service, the police, the courts, the monarchy, the church, industry, the trade unions, charities. Particularly after 1960 the list expanded to represent a more pluralist establishment, and altered in tone to present some issues as more personality-based, but this remained fundamentally what one critic has called 'institutional news'.

Journalists 'just *knew*' what their audiences wanted (Westminster Press chief executive Hew Stevenson's description of Harold Evans' editorship of the *Northern Echo*). Stevenson, speaking in 1990, argued that 'good editors . . . know in their bones what kind of paper they are trying to produce'. Leslie Sellers, a former production editor of the *Daily Mail* and author of the most celebrated (and most consulted) book on sub-editing, said that the journalist's first duty was '**TO APPROACH EVERY STORY FROM THE POINT OF VIEW OF THE READER**' (*The Simple Subs Book*, 1968 – emphasis in original). How? Sellers' preference was to develop 'a good general knowledge' from reading newspapers, and to watch television to keep up with 'popular' culture. News, of course, was only one ingredient of the media. Other elements, including advertising, played a role in fulfilling the Reithian objective of educating, informing and entertaining audiences. The prime duty of journalism was to provide information in response to what it discerned to be the interests of its audiences. PRIME MINISTER SACKS CABINET was without doubt a story of importance: whether it made the papers or appeared on broadcast news depended on whether, in the journalists' view, audiences were interested in it. In turn that hinged on the paper's (or, more rarely, programme's) target audience, and the journalists' 'instinctive' understanding of that audience. 'News,' said Sellers, 'is not an abstraction'.

The most common expression of putting the news in context was contained in the notion of proximity: sacked Cabinets at Westminster were presumed to be of interest everywhere in the United Kingdom; sacked Cabinets in Washington, or Delhi, of interest to fewer British people. Individual media had identified and tried to exploit their own markets; but there was seen to be only one market for fundamentally the same *types* of news. In the 1960s, therefore, it was still possible for *The Times* in particular to be considered a paper of record, and the BBC the transmitter of a national news agenda. Variation came in the interpretation of the level of interest of specific audiences in individual news items. The death of a child in a gas explosion in Derbyshire, Sellers pointed out, would have been a major story in the local weekly paper; a small front-page story in the regional evening; a few paragraphs on an inside page of the national dailies; and not worth a mention in a Swedish or German paper. Twenty years later, Gareth Weekes, the editor of the weekly *Salisbury Journal*, said

> 'World-shattering events could be happening in Devizes . . . but not a line would appear in the *Salisbury Journal*, because our world ends at the village of Upavon.'

This kind of approach was increasingly questioned from the 1960s onwards.

First, the interests of the media began to diverge: radio and television were better able to meet the criteria (outlined above) for 'hard' and 'important' news. A survey discovered that the papers which tapped into the new emerging popular interest in television (in the early 1960s, the *Daily Mirror*) were most likely to attract readers. So, 'soft' news about television programmes and soap opera stars (as well as television listings) began to appear more frequently in the press. Alongside this, the media began relying on more sophisticated (and perhaps more reliable) methods than journalistic intuition and interpretation to determine what mattered to audiences. In 1964 the *Daily Herald* was relaunched as *The Sun* on the back of market research, and in 1971 the *Daily Mail* changed to tabloid format and was targeted specifically at women. The research appeared to show that what people wanted were more human interest stories and entertainment-related features. James Curran (*Power Without Responsibility*) calculated that over the 30 years up to 1976 the amount of public affairs coverage in the 'popular' papers declined by 50 per cent – and by up to two-thirds in some cases. By the end of the period that kind of news took up less space than sport.

It was, above all, the success of *The Sun* ('soaraway', is how the paper described it) which seemed to confirm the validity of the new approach. Under its first editor, Larry Lamb, it both matched (and beat) its direct rival the *Daily Mirror* in quantity of orthodox news stories carried (although each was often reduced to a single paragraph), and usurped the *Mirror*'s role as the newspaper of television. Lamb believed that television was 'the biggest single area of human interest'. One effect was to divide journalism. The difference between the 'quality' papers, which still pursued a more 'serious' news agenda, and the tabloids seemed to widen. Throughout the 1980s there was constant debate over the value of a news agenda which seemed to concentrate almost exclusively on soap opera actors, the Royal Family and sex scandals. As more newspapers began subscribing to that agenda, so the excesses appeared to multiply: stories were unjustifiably elaborated, and even fabricated. The scramble for market share, rather than journalistic values, seemed to predominate. A *Sun* journalist who invented a conversation with the widow of a soldier killed in the Falklands was actually later promoted to an editorship. The 'quality' press and broadcasting found it difficult to stay aloof. First they were drawn into reporting the behaviour of the tabloid press as the issue of the standards of journalism became a matter for public debate. Soon, however, they appeared at least to be partially sharing the 'new' news agenda.

While debates about news values seemed most naturally to be confined to newspapers and television and radio news, they had their repercussions in other media, too. In the 1980s two traditional weekly women's magazines, *Woman's Own* and *Woman*, adopted a more tabloid approach, and in 1988 the Spanish 'news magazine' *Hola!* was launched in a British edition as the weekly *Hello!*, specialising in celebrity interviews. The more up-market monthly, *Marie Claire*, which first appeared in Britain in the same year, traded, Louise Chunn noted in the *Guardian*, on 'the promise of salacious stories' and 'first-person shockers'. In the early 1990s a number of such magazines regularly featured explicit articles and photographs on sex, provoking considerable debate about whether the sudden upsurge in interest in the topic was altruistic or driven by concerns over circulation during an economic recession. The cross-fertilisation of the media (particularly, the role of *The Sun* in setting standards) was noted by a number of commentators. Women's magazines, it seemed, were not exempt from the process of 'tabloidisation'.

10

'GOOD NEWS' VERSUS 'BAD NEWS'

For many the 'tabloidisation' of the news agenda led not only to a change in the relationship between the 'important' and the 'interesting' (decisively in favour of the latter), but also to a severe narrowing of the definition of both. Traditional 'hard' news had to fulfil *in extremis* the criteria listed in Chapter 9 to make the paragraph *The Sun* was prepared to devote to it: wars had to be more brutal, murders more depraved, disasters more catastrophic. The BBC television journalist Martyn Lewis complained in 1993 that too much 'good news' was simply going unreported in favour of a diet of 'conflict and criticism'. News values, he claimed, were based 'on the extent to which things go wrong. The bigger the tragedy, the greater the images of the disaster, the more prominence it requires.' In television the time had come, he said, 'to change the journalistic judgement of the people who shape [news] programmes, so they treat bad and good stories with equal seriousness and enthusiasm'. A similar debate had already taken place in America, where the major television networks had been subject to a great deal of public criticism for overly concentrating on 'bad news'. It was predictable, then, that Lewis would receive a large amount of support from the British public. Even the prime minister, John Major, argued that 'people . . . want the good news as well'.

Although some prominent journalists also supported him, the majority were hostile. Most expressed fears about news management, and manipulation by propagandists. Editorial primacy, they felt, was in danger of being eroded. John Cole, a former BBC political editor and senior *Guardian* journalist, argued, however, that it was the public support which the cause of 'good news' had elicited that was dangerous. New values were not to be set by public opinion: 'News,' he wrote, 'must be judged by whether it is right, interesting and significant . . .' The suspicion had been raised that, as it now faced competition from satellite television and a reorganised ITN, both of which, it was felt, were more prone to 'tabloidisation', the BBC would pursue a more populist news agenda. To *The Independent*, however, the debate had raised fundamental issues of the relationship between journalists and their audiences: a leading article said,

> 'Senior journalists and television producers are apt to believe that proper, grown-up (and, usually, male) reporters should be concerned only with "hard" news, comprising war, disaster and crime, or with exposure . . . The rest of human life is for women and boys . . . however, there is widespread public sympathy for Mr Lewis. The professionals, instead of mocking, should be worried that they are so out of touch with readers and viewers.'
>
> 2 May 1993

Were journalistic news values being challenged by new public perceptions of what was 'important' and 'interesting', and which had primacy; or had journalists made the wrong presumptions all along? Whatever the answers to those questions (and they were by no means obvious), as Lewis pointed out, the act of confronting their existence alone was proving painful to journalists.

By the time Lewis spoke out, many provincial newspapers had already embarked on 'good news' experiments. For at least a decade, and faced with rapidly declining readerships (see Chapter 7), the provincial daily papers in particular had made strenuous attempts to emulate the success *The Sun* had enjoyed among the national press. During the 1980s large numbers adopted the tabloid format, both in size and in content. When Matthew Engel surveyed a sample of evening papers in England and Wales, he found an unremitting diet of 'Panic, Scare, Horror, Shock, Anger'. He noted that 'in these papers the roll of horror often seems relentless, page after page', amounting to 'the drip, drip, drip of years of distortion' (*Guardian*, 22 March 1993). Those who bore a large share of responsibility for this, he argued, were journalists wedded to traditional 'hard' news values. Alex Spillus, criticising the standard of journalism in London's weekly press, observed

'The news pages are dominated by have-a-go heroes, sex beasts and vicious attackers. Hyperbolism and huge headlines rule OK.'
Evening Standard (18 January 1993)

The linking of structural decline and news values led to a bout of reappraisal by almost all the individual major provincial publishing groups, the Newspaper Society and a number of researchers in the 1990s. The consensus was that local journalists had lost touch with their readers. Research conducted by the Henley Centre and the University of Central Lancashire indicated that journalists' traditional news values were no longer shared by significant numbers of the public. The reasons were cultural: demographic changes and altered work and leisure patterns had resulted in a shattering of old values and habits, which had not been accurately reflected in the editorial columns of provincial newspapers. In many instances established geographical communities had broken up, and new communities of interest had formed. Newspapers which inhabited what Stuart Garner, the editorial director of TRN, called 'shock–horror clichédom' were failing to satisfy either. Journalists themselves argued that if they had lost touch it was because reductions in staff and other cost-cutting by managements had left them overstretched, desk-bound and unable to fulfil their traditional role in the community. Engel noted that many evening newspapers printed so early that the journalists had little time to report much more than the crimes, road traffic accidents and fires given to them each morning by the emergency services. The NUJ regarded attempts to reform news values as designed simply to attract more advertising.

Two broad approaches to re-assessing news values emerged among the provincial press for dealing with the situation. Led by TRN, many newspapers opted to pursue the new communities forming around lifestyle choices. News values were focused around consumerism. This was reflected in a celebrated instance in 1991 when the TRN newspaper, the *Evening Chronicle* in Newcastle chose as its main story, not the discovery of a body in a city alley, but a price 'war' between supermarkets. Other papers started regular features listing the comparative prices in shops. The idea, TRN maintained, was to 'ease back on hard news'. News columns could be devoted to 'recipes, health tips, quizzes, puzzles, info-lines, school term dates, calendar events, bye-laws, opening times of swimming baths, railway station and taxi telephone numbers and start a lost pets column' (*The Key*). Sophisticated market research and reader databases began to be used to target specialist interest groups: the *Oxford Mail* was one paper which claimed to have used these techniques successfully. One criticism of this approach was that, by chiefly targeting individual consumers, it was driving the provincial press away from its traditional mass market.

The answer, some felt, was to return to the broad-based community news values which had characterised the provincial press before 'tabloidisation' and when it had been properly regarded as 'local'. The results of the Henley research indicated that the more successful weekly papers were actively involved in their communities, running campaigns, sponsoring local events, publishing many readers' letters and promoting their journalists. The Central Lancashire research also revealed that many newspapers favoured a return to traditional local journalism, emphasising the detailed coverage of purely local affairs. Alan Prosser went further and argued that local newspaper editors, who he accused of wimpishness, should rediscover a 'sense of social mission', and not only get involved in but instigate local controversy. None of these issues looked capable of quick resolution. Could journalists get the balance right between 'good' and 'bad', 'important' and 'interesting' news, or had the power structures within the media, between owners, journalists and audiences, changed to their disadvantage? What had caused such questions to be raised was the re-assertion in the 1980s of market forces.

The market seemed arguably to have most impact on television. It raised questions about the role of journalism in television which compelled journalists to rediscover justifications for their work. In response to the twin challenges of the 'mission to explain', instituted by the director general, John Birt, at the BBC, and an intimation by the ITV network centre that it was looking for 'new types of factual programmes', journalists felt it necessary to defend their record of producing 'serious' coverage of 'important' subjects which still appealed to viewers. Granada's current affairs programme, World in Action, its former head Ray Fitzwalter claimed, had broadcast 'strong programmes of interest to millions'. Paul Woolwich, the last editor of Thames Television's This Week, argued,

> 'We take on the big issues, the major stories of the day, and make them more palatable, using flair and imagination – if necessary, a gimmick. This is not popularist television, it's popularised television.'

There remained a widespread belief that a substantial audience existed for what Martin McNamara, of *UK Press Gazette*, identified as 'strong, interesting, mainstream, serious current affairs'. Claudia Milne, the executive producer, promised that Twenty/Twenty's Seven Days, a successor to This Week, would focus on 'hard journalism that breaks stories which have a relevance to viewers', while Charles Tremayne, executive producer of World in Action, undertook to continue making 'challenging, factual programming that gets an audience'. At the BBC Colin Adams, head of broadcasting in the North, emphasised the worth to the ratings of 'trusted journalism', and Tony Hall, the corporation's director of news and current affairs, argued that 'there are accessible, good ways of getting across . . . information'.

The Birt and ITV strategies were most commonly represented as forming a kind of pincer movement around TV journalism – the over-analytical and inaccessible attacking from the left, while tabloid television closed in on the right – with orthodox journalism – informative, campaigning, exploratory, challenging – being squeezed into a small, insecure redoubt. Explanation, as defined by Birt, seemed overly dense and unattractive; while tabloid television, as envisioned at ITV, was vacuous entertainment. There seemed to be no common ground between them. Journalists argued, however, that traditionally journalism struck the balance between being informative and analytical, and entertaining and accessible. The question was where was the balance to be struck?

The London News Network, which provided news programmes for the London ITV companies Carlton and London Weekend, adopted a news-and-features tabloid approach modelled on the *Daily Mirror* and *Daily Mail* which aimed to be 'informative but not boring'. A further development of the format had been promised by Moses Znaimer, a member of the Channel 5 bid consortium, whose CityTV experience in Toronto appeared to have led him to want to break down the boundaries between 'information' and 'entertainment'. Adhering to old notions of the strict separation of news from entertainment, Bruce Gyngell, the head of TV-am, argued, amounted to nothing more than 'cultural snobbery'. Nevertheless, attempts to blur the distinctions generally met with hostility from journalists, even though 'straight' TV journalism had long adopted an entertainment–information synergy; for example, World in Action devised the dramadocumentary format. There were widespread fears of an invasion of 'infotainment'. By 1994, *UK Press Gazette* observed, 'almost any excuse to abuse ITV's factual output is leapt upon'.

Uncertainty about what was news, and the role of news struck at the core of journalism. Traditionally journalists had largely predetermined the news for their audiences. Little thought was given to the use value of news: it was presumed that if events were firstly 'important' and then of 'interest', the news they engendered amounted to useful (and perhaps entertaining) information. The playwright Tom Gallacher, writing in the *Journalist's Handbook*, argued that while 'information is of *use*' (original emphasis), 'News, on the other hand, . . . is a luxury concern for those who can afford to busy their minds with what is none of their concern . . .'. He went on,

> '. . . the sensational tabloid papers are much nearer to offering a general public service than their pompous brothers. The service is entertainment. And, for the great mass of the public, the only entertainment which can be had merely by reading must include: titillation, sex scandal, gossip, vicarious enjoyment of a lubricious life-style, reported wealth and crime.'

In the 1980s most journalists would have been extremely uncomfortable to find themselves relocated in show business. By the early 1990s many were already there, writing daily updates on the plots of television soap operas and paying enormous sums of money for anodyne interviews with celebrities. Some were becoming marketers of 'useful information' on the opening hours of chemist's shops and how to survive in a snow storm. Yet there also seemed to be a role for more orthodox journalism. In 1986 *The Independent* was launched with a strenuous belief in traditional journalism. At the BBC Birt's commitment was to more analytical and explanatory news. It was not certain that either would prevail. *The Independent* had to sell a controlling share-holding to Mirror Group Newspapers (MGN). The BBC continued to confront an increase in competitor broadcasters leading to a decline in its share of both television and radio audiences which might yet derail Birtism. Whether the intrusion of more raw market forces in the 1980s had led to a more genuine expression of popular taste, or had simply facilitated crass commercialism was a moot point. In any event, the cornerstone of journalism, news, had been dislodged, and it was more difficult than perhaps it had been for 100 years to be precise about what news was in practice. Many of the characteristics listed at the beginning of Chapter 9 were clearly much less evident: news was less reactive (and more proactive, as papers and programmes set their own agendas); it was less 'important' (and more 'interesting'); it was less concerned with community (and more with life-style). There was less 'hard' news and more 'soft' news. Attempts were being made, especially in the provincial press, to rely less on 'institutional news', and to get closer to the reader. And perhaps there was an inclination to be less negative and shocking. Many journalists undoubtedly found this repulsive and a negation of their professional values. In 1989 *UK Press Gazette* warned that there was a danger that 'the essential importance of what is produced – news – is beginning to get lost . . .'. No journalist, however, could ignore the fundamental shift which this reappraisal of the worth of news represented.

11

OBJECTIVITY

> 'Once a newspaper touches a story, the facts are lost forever, even to the protagonists.'
>
> Norman Mailer,
> *The Presidential Papers* (1963)

Journalists in the twentieth century have commonly perceived their first responsibility to be to fairness and accuracy. This arose out of two closely related concerns: with professional standards, and with the idea of journalism as a public service. Journalists strove to 'tell it as it is'. They dealt above all else in facts, and presented the facts objectively. This ideal was represented in the much used mining metaphor: journalists *dug* for the facts (often described as *nuggets* of information) which lay hidden until they brought them *to light*. Regardless of the consequences, the journalist's prime duty was discovery and revelation. This placed a premium on accuracy, as inaccurate information was effectively of no public use. Moreover, the facts had to be presented without consideration of interest – frankly, fearlessly and freely, as one national newspaper used to claim. Journalists were fond of appropriating the Duke of Wellington's remark that they were called upon to 'Publish and be damned'.

Objectivity was both an expression of the journalistic ideal, and a journalistic method. Journalists strove to be objective to ensure that the facts emerged untainted, as Scott put it (see Chapter 2), and to sustain public confidence in journalism. Objectivity was the 'key' and the 'cornerstone', as it has been described, of the ethos of journalism. It came to be associated with a list of characteristics which exemplified 'good' journalism:

- truthfulness
- fairness
- impartiality
- non-partisanship
- a lack of bias
- neutrality
- balance
- a lack of distortion

As we have seen (Chapters 9 and 10), at least by the 1990s the public view was at considerable variance with that of journalism orthodoxy. Newspaper journalism in particular was regarded as both biased and untruthful.

Three main arguments developed against the idea of objective journalism:

1. that journalism *couldn't* be objective

2. that it *wasn't* objective

3. that it *shouldn't* be objective

1. Distortion and partiality, it has been argued, are built into the actual practices of journalism. Material is selected and presented according to 'news' criteria dependent on subjective judgements (described in Chapter 9). Facts are not all equal, but carry specific values. That begged the question of how 'truthful' the facts were. In a notorious incident following the Hillsborough football stadium disaster in 1989 *The Sun* printed allegations that drunken Liverpool fans had obstructed the police and rescuers at the scene. The story was headed THE TRUTH. Nevertheless, the account was immediately refuted by people in Liverpool who burnt copies of the paper, while newsagents refused to sell it. News (facts, the truth) varied and reflected what either journalists or audiences (or both) thought was important, or interesting, or of meaning.

2. To some extent, a development of this argument was that which claimed that in practice journalism was demonstrably biased. Researchers, such as the Glasgow University Media Group in Britain which studied television news in the 1970s and 1980s, and Noam Chomsky and Ed Herman in America, concluded that overall journalism supported the *status quo*. What they called the dominant values and interests of society were given prominence, and alternative views were marginalised.

Besides, even at an individual level, it was highly improbable that all journalists could suppress their own biases all the time.

3. Given the two arguments above, why should journalists try to be objective? Should they not acknowledge their personal and collective biases, and the social and cultural value systems within which they work? Is there anything wrong with what has been called 'commitment journalism'? For a start, a great deal of journalism *is* opinionated: the idea of objectivity has traditionally applied chiefly to news reporting, and not feature writing, which contained comment and analysis. Second, taking points 1 and 2 above together, the pretence of objectivity has simply given precedence and credence to 'dominant' views over alternative beliefs. Thus objective journalism has failed in its declared purpose of firstly serving the public interest.

The development of a public service ethos in broadcasting from the 1920s may be seen as an attempt to resolve the disputes arising from these debates. Lord Reith saw the BBC as 'a powerful means of promoting social unity' through a reflection of the variety of views and opinions held in British society. The role of broadcasting (it was also imposed on independent television and radio from the 1950s) was to present these views impartially and in a balanced manner. British broadcasters were forbidden to support one cause or another: instead they were to act as neutral conduits for the opinions of others. Yet what overlay this was a prior claim of the national interest. This was exemplified by the position the BBC found itself in during the Falklands War in 1982, when it was attacked by government ministers for adopting a stance of supposed neutrality in its reporting of the conflict. The duty of British broadcasting, the government argued, was first and foremost to support Britain. In addition, broadcasters themselves have rejected the idea of absolute impartiality, and have accepted that they have not remained neutral when it has come to matters of truth, justice, and legality.

It would appear necessary to separate the journalistic ideal of objectivity from other concepts such as impartiality, neutrality, balance, and truthfulness. Objectivity may itself be partial, biased and unbalanced. Facts, the journalist Claud Cockburn observed, do not lie about 'like pieces of gold ore . . . waiting to be picked up . . .'. The process of writing a story has usually begun with the journalist, who then sought out the facts to fit the story. This, Cockburn added, was tantamount to admitting that 'the truth does not matter . . . [and] that journalism is a way of "cooking" the facts'. Objectivity then has come to have a much narrower practical definition. Following the public service broadcasting model, objective journalism has sought to 'give . . . voice' to different sides of the story. The reader is left to 'judge the truth', according to the American academic Judith Lichtenberg ('In defense of objectivity', 1991). She added, however,

> 'As a journalistic virtue, then, objectivity requires that reporters do not let their preconceptions cloud their vision. It doesn't mean they see nothing, or that their findings may not be significant and controversial.'

The journalist's task was to 'come to a conclusion based on a reasoned evaluation of the evidence' rather than being 'biased toward that conclusion from the start'.

This approach stressed the need for journalists to source stories. Objective journalism devalued the role of the journalist who, in the words of the American journalist A. J. Liebling, 'writes what he (*sic*) sees'. In the 1970s there was an increasing tendency for the British press to carry interpretative reporting, in which journalists underpinned their first-hand accounts with attempts to explain their meaning, and towards specialist reporting, in which journalists speculated on the meaning of events. Some critics have seen this as creating confusion between 'facts' and 'comment'. At the same time, to make their interpretations authoritative, journalists relied on credible sources for both 'facts' and commentary. Such sources were more likely to be found in so-called official circles – the government, political parties, the civil service, police, the military. This gave these institutional sources a powerful say in the shaping of news.

The danger was that such arrangements facilitated news management. Credible sources were able, if they wished, to circulate baseless and even outrageous ideas. It was alleged that the lobby system, in which accredited journalists in the House of Commons were given briefings by the government on the understanding that they would not reveal their sources, was sometimes used in this way. Similarly, British military commanders planted 'black propaganda' in the press during the emergency in Northern Ireland in the 1970s. Journalists who sought to challenge what they believed to be misinformation were often restricted to balancing one view with another, leaving the audience to judge the veracity of competing versions of the same event. By the late 1980s there was little room in the British media for journalists to make 'a reasoned evaluation of the evidence'.

OBJECTIVITY

According to many analyses, investigative journalism, where this had most naturally occurred, went into steep decline, particularly in the press, after 1979. Objective journalism had become less the testing and challenging of presumption, orthodoxy and the 'official view'. To some extent this tradition continued only in television. Thames Television's current affairs programme This Week broadcast an investigation in 1988 which directly contradicted the official version of how British security forces had shot dead a number of Irish people in Gibraltar presumed to be terrorists planting a bomb. This led to a vilification of the programme and its makers, orchestrated in part by official sources, but given voice chiefly by the press. This led to the rather incongruous situation of the *Sunday Times*, which under its previous owners had built a reputation for investigative reporting, attacking such journalism in television.

At the same time, the growing use of market research to identify audience needs and expectations also began to undermine journalists' ideas of objectivity. The Reithian notion of public service, embodied in the promotion of 'a cultural, moral and educative force for the improvement of knowledge, taste and manners . . .', seemed to be breaking down in the face of the demand for entertainment, titillation and trivia. 'The problems of objectivity,' Lichtenberg argued, 'are political . . .'

Nevertheless, research conducted in the 1970s and 1980s indicated the extent to which public service journalism continued to offer opportunities to articulate alternative views. This was most evident in broadcasting. Two studies, of the coverage of terrorism and of defence, concluded that television news and current affairs and documentary programmes did not completely ignore opinions which differed from the dominant view. Similarly, it was noted elsewhere that credible alternative sources existed alongside powerful official sources, and were used by journalists to authenticate their reports. At a national level organisations such as Oxfam and Greenpeace were seen as having established an 'alternative' credibility: on the more local level, residents' organisations, action campaigns by parents, and protest groups often enjoyed access to the media on a par with institutional bodies.

The most obvious expression of such voices was the 'alternative' press. From the 1960s until 1980 these newspapers and magazines were overwhelmingly political and radical in intent. Their content, however, differed. Some were community-based, others addressed their readers' life-styles. Few, if any, were commercially viable. On the one hand, their existence indicated that they filled a gap in the market left by the conventional press. On the other hand, their inability to make money meant that there was no real market in the gap. Some successfully bridged the gap. The best known example was *Time Out* which achieved considerable commercial success by abandoning its radical politics in favour of listings. Others, such as the feminist magazine *Spare Rib*, which finally closed in 1993, stuck to their original objectives.

In 1980 there were more than 70 local alternative papers in the United Kingdom. By 1994 the number had fallen to two. Many simply ran out of steam. Commercialism did not guarantee survival. *Rochdale's Alternative Paper*, which published between 1971 and 1983, led to a printing co-operative which by 1994 had a £2 million turnover and 50 employees. The *Northern Star*, started in 1974 as *Leeds Other Paper*, folded twenty years later after converting to a listings magazine. Of the two survivors, one, the *West Highland Free Press* on the Isle of Skye, was primarily a local newspaper, carrying 'soft' news as well as more investigative political stories.

As this alternative press declined, however, another took its place. By 1994 there were about 250 football fanzines in circulation. Andrew Hobbs, a founder and co-editor of the *Preston Other Paper*, believed that

'Fanzines have many similarities with the alternative papers of the 70s. They arose spontaneously to fill a gap left by other media, are done for love not money, and are part of a culture which supports and values their efforts.'
UK Press Gazette (24 January 1994)

Other new non-mainstream publications (some commercially successful, some not) included *Viz* and *Scallywag*; a number of titles for gay and lesbian audiences; papers, magazines and a news agency specialising in 'alternative' views of the so-called third world, and *The Big Issue*, a weekly sold by homeless people with a circulation in 1994 of 150,000. Opportunities for alternative broadcasting have been more limited, although there were experiments in feminist and community radio.

The impact on the mainstream media has been considerable. Magazines such as *Private Eye* have broken stories followed up by the Fleet Street press, television and radio. The local radical press has forced mainstream evening and weekly papers to give more coverage to community issues and groups. The alternative media have often acted as an antidote to mainstream media complacency.

Photography

> 'Photography has a validity which is, for most of us, synonymous with truth. "Photography cannot lie" was a well-known and much-quoted maxim right from the time of the discovery of the process. Even now this belief still lingers, even though we know that photography can lie and lie very convincingly. Yet we still have a tendency, even a compulsion, to trust the veracity of a photographic image.'
>
> Jorge Lewinski,
> *The Camera At War: War Photography from 1848 to the Present Day* (London, 1978)

The idea that the camera does not lie reached a new dimension with the primacy of television news. The cameras appeared to transport the viewer, sometimes 'live', to the actual scene of events. Even more than newspaper photographs, film and video footage seemed to offer 'a simple equivalent to reality' and, for journalists, 'proof of authenticity'. The specific 'objectivity of photography' provided a 'bedrock of truth' (John Taylor, *War Photography: Realism in the British Press* [London, 1991]). Quite apart from the theoretical arguments that photographic *realism* must not be confused with *reality*, as Lewinski pointed out, photographs have clearly lied.

Photography has been susceptible to faking, trickery, manipulation and misrepresentation. Events apparently snapped at the moment of occurrence turned out to be reconstructions staged specifically for the camera. Depictions of apparent drama proved to be calculated representations acted out for filming. Pictures of one thing have been passed off as showing something quite different. Misrepresenting the event or the image, however, has remained relatively rare. Manipulation has been much more common, and indeed has formed a central part of the technique of photo-journalism. Harold Evans, in what became a standard textbook on the subject (*Pictures on a Page: Photo-journalism, Graphics and Picture Editing* [London, 1978]), argued that this might be 'acceptable in order to improve innocuous illustration'. Most photographs used by the mainstream media, and particularly fashion shots and magazine cover illustrations, are systematically re-touched and 'enhanced'. Re-touching has been used for more sinister reasons, though: a photograph taken in 1917 of Lenin addressing a crowd with Leon Trotsky standing beside the podium was later circulated with

Trotsky painted out, in accordance with his status as a non-person in the Stalinist Soviet Union.

Nevertheless, Evans was more concerned with another common practice – the creation of photo-montages in which one image is produced from piecing together bits of two or more photographs. Montages have normally been made to improve the dramatic composition of a picture by bringing the main protagonists closer together. They have also been used, however, to 'prove' the presence of someone who, it was suspected, was not actually there when the photograph was supposedly taken. In February 1994 the North Korean news agency circulated a picture apparently of chairman Kim Il-sung and his son, Kim Jong-il, on the North Korean-Chinese border. Most Western news organisations believed the picture to be a fake, composed of three separate photographs – of the landscape and the two men, taken at different times. (In 1994 Kim Jong-il was thought to be either dead or critically ill.) 'At their most devilish' photo-montages, Evans warned, 'can . . . create a lampoon of incongruity or a lie'.

In June 1993 *The Sun* had a photograph of a 55-year-old monk with a woman 30 years his junior with whom he was said to have been emotionally involved. First, the paper 'moved' the two people closer together. Then it arranged for one of its own photographers to be photographed wearing a monk's habit. Finally, the picture of the photographer's body (in the habit) was superimposed on the photograph of the monk. The result was a front-page picture apparently showing the monk in his habit shoulder-to-shoulder with the woman. The paper's argument was that the manipulated image made the essential facts of the story clearer for readers. The picture editor of the *Observer*, Tony McGrath, condemned unacknowledged manipulation of photographs as unethical. 'It's a fix,' he said, 'and should not be allowed' (*UK Press Gazette*, 5 July 1993).

A major concern was the ease with which photographs could be manipulated using computers – 'child's play', according to the *Guardian*. That paper's picture editor, Eamonn McCabe, estimated that an untrained operator could learn the technique in an hour. A reasonably powerful computer, a scanner and off-the-shelf software, together costing about £10,000, would allow almost unlimited manipulation of photographs. Photo-montages were seen as one way of providing more 'reader friendly' imagery, and it was forecast that their use would become more common. One consequence of this, it was felt, was that the whole process of picture editing would become more obvious, and as a result might undermine belief in photographic 'truth'. The extent to which photographs in the normal course of editing were altered (through scaling, cropping, and reversing as well as retouching), and made to illustrate the stories they accompanied, could turn them into something quite different from what had originally been shot. Many journalists feared that the integrity of photography would be compromised, and argued for voluntary regulation of photo-manipulation.

Journalists' defence of objectivity (in both the written word and in photography) should be seen perhaps not as a claim to neutrality or impartiality, or to a single version of 'the truth', but more as an attempt to defend professional practice. Objectivity has underwritten the value of journalism as founded in investigation, evaluation and presentation of 'the facts'. Any abandonment of objectivity has been seen as a retreat from 'honest journalism'.

12

ETHICS

> 'The paper has always faced up
> to the fact that most people's
> basic interests are not politics,
> philosophy or economics. They are
> more likely to be money, sex, crime,
> sport, food, drink and what's on telly.'
>
> Roslyn Grose,
> *The 'Sun'-sation* (London, 1989)

> 'Journalists have been forced to be more
> ethical because it is very difficult to
> expose politicians for lying and then
> turn around and lie yourself.'
>
> David Shaw,
> *Los Angeles Times*

Journalists' adherence to ideas of accuracy and fairness in what they do has led almost inevitably to a central concern with the regulation of practice. Because journalism has remained a formally unregulated occupation, unlike medicine or the law, there has been no authority to draw up guidelines for journalists to work within, and to sit in judgement on allegations of misbehaviour. Journalists in the United Kingdom have never enjoyed substantial special privileges in law: they have been regarded as ordinary private individuals, subject to the full range of legal rights and responsibilities. Throughout the twentieth century governments have made a virtue of limiting State interference. Journalism, therefore, has been largely self-regulating on a voluntary and chiefly *ad hoc* basis. A more systematic approach has been adopted with broadcasting, which was subject to statutory requirements from the outset, and following the establishment of the Press Council in 1947. Nevertheless regulation was primarily of the media rather than journalism directly. Only the NCTJ (as described in Chapter 13) addressed standards in journalism specifically.

Journalists worked to vague and far from universal rules-of-thumb dictated variously by the law, employers, the Press Council, public opinion, and the NUJ and other professional bodies. Standards not only varied (for example, between broadcasting and the press, and between the quality and the popular papers), but they also changed. In the 1960s in particular there were widespread complaints about the perceived extreme liberalism and sensationalism of some journalism. Journalists were often seen as being at the forefront of the 'social revolution'. At the same time, the 1967 Criminal Justice Act imposed unprecedented restrictions on the reporting of court cases which many journalists saw as a major breach of the principle of open justice. Five years earlier, the journalist's presumed 'right' to protect sources of information was declared to be contempt of court, and two journalists were jailed for refusing to divulge their sources.

The main mechanism for formulating and articulating journalists' responses to such developments, and for discussing standards of practice more generally, was the NUJ, which by the late 1970s represented about 90 per cent of British journalists. Its membership included editors as well as the mass of ordinary working journalists. The union had a binding code of conduct for members (see Figure 12.1 at the end of this chapter). For the most part journalists shared a broad but definable set of values founded on an ideology of calling the core of which was the journalist's traditional news values. Journalists strove to get the news to the public, fairly and accurately, and within the bounds of good taste. What constituted news, fairness, accuracy and good taste was determined for the most part by the judgement of peers and public opinion.

In the 1980s the situation changed quite markedly, as a result primarily of the enormously enhanced competitiveness among the tabloid press for a declining readership (see Chapter 7). The competition for readers, as Roy Greenslade, an editor of the *Daily Mirror* during this period, noted in 1994, compelled journalists to publish stories which they would otherwise have regarded as unfit for publication. Moreover, the desire to secure such material ahead of their rivals led to both an increase in the practice of paying people for their stories (so-called 'cheque-book journalism') and a growing disregard for the privacy of individuals. What was seen as the need to make such stories more and more sensational led to a concentration on sex, royalty and the rich and famous (and, where possible, all three together), and eventually to instances of pure fabrication. Caroline Wyatt, herself a BBC journalist, recalled how a feature article she wrote for *The Independent on Sunday* about tracing her birth father and mother in Australia, unleashed 'the hounds of tabloid TV and press'. Newspapers bid against each other for her story. One tried to bribe her to break her contract with a rival. A journalist threatened to make up a story if she didn't co-operate and provide information. The BBC brought her natural parents to London for a 'live' reunion on air without warning and against her wishes. She wrote later,

> 'By this time I was beginning to feel a distinct loathing for the words "journalist", "contract" or "exclusive" . . . Almost all the coverage of the story contained sloppy writing, errors and a large proportion of fantasy . . . it had simply not occurred to . . . me that a small story could generate so much interest and, to a certain extent, intrusion . . . it was enlightening to be on the other side of the fence, and to realise quite how pushy, cynical and insincere some journalists can be.'
>
> '"Love for sale! Love for sale!"' (1994)

There seemed to be little or nothing to prevent such cases, or worse, happening. The public appetite for this kind of story appeared insatiable. *The Sun*, which was deemed to be the specialist in this area, was also the most commercially successful newspaper of the 1980s. As the decade progressed into the 1990s, the tabloid press indulged in frenzied bouts of gossip- and sleaze-mongering about the famous, the royal family and politicians. The Press Council was widely regarded as ineffectual. The NUJ withdrew from it and in 1986 established its own elected ethics council; but this ran into difficulties immediately as many journalists objected to what a former general secretary of the union called 'persecuting' members 'for doing their job'. Many of those disciplined for breaches of the code of conduct simply resigned from the union. In any event, the NUJ was being derecognised by many employers and losing both members and authority. Perhaps most significantly, from the mid-1970s many newspaper editors had left the union. There seemed no longer to be any consensus on journalism standards, nor a body to impose any standards.

Four times between 1987 and 1989 attempts were made by individual MPs to introduce legislation to impose constraints on the press. In

1988 the government issued its own warning that some form of statutory control might be unavoidable if newspapers did not put their house in order, and the following year it set up a Committee on Privacy chaired by David Calcutt. Three cases in particular had served to begin to change the public mood: the libelling of the singer Elton John by *The Sun*, the photographing and interviewing the actor Gorden Kaye as he lay seriously ill in hospital after an accident, and *The Sun*'s reporting of the Hillsborough disaster (see Chapter 11). The Calcutt Report recommended no fundamental changes, only a strengthening of voluntary self-regulation through the replacement of the Press Council by a body working to a formal code of practice.

The Press Complaints Commission (PCC) began work in 1991 with a code drawn up by national newspaper editors (see Figure 12.2 at the end of this chapter). It did not curb the excesses of tabloid journalism. In the summer and autumn of 1992 there were revelations about the state of the marriage of the Prince and Princess of Wales, and of an affair between the minister responsible for the press, David Mellor, and the actress Antonia de Sancha; photographs of the Duchess of York sunbathing topless in the south of France with her financial adviser, and transcripts of telephone conversations, first between Princess Diana and a male friend, and then, Prince Charles and Lady Camilla Parker-Bowles. This more or less coincided with the expiry of the PCC's initial probationary period, and Calcutt was asked to provide another review. In January 1993 he recommended legislation to establish a press tribunal in place of the PCC, and to outlaw certain intrusions onto private property by journalists, including the use of telephoto lenses and bugging devices. The National Heritage Select Committee, which reported in March 1993 after holding hearings on privacy and media intrusion, also favoured legislative action involving, among other things, a press ombudsman, fines and a protection of privacy act.

The government was reportedly deeply divided over the issue, and by the summer of 1994 proposals for legislation, originally expected in September 1993, had apparently been postponed indefinitely. In general, the government's inclination was to avoid legislative press controls if at all possible. The PCC seized the opportunity provided by the hiatus to meet some of the complaints that it was no more effective than the old Press Council. It introduced a majority of lay members, and opened up a 'hot line' for complaints. A special privacy commissioner was appointed. Newspapers began writing the code of practice into the contracts of journalists, and editors in particular were said to be bound by its terms and liable to dismissal for breaking them. *The Sun* introduced a code specifically for freelance journalists contributing to the paper: it opened with the statement that accuracy was 'the first and foremost requirement for journalism in the 1990s'.

Yet decisively, public opinion hardened further. When the *Sunday Mirror* published photographs taken surreptitiously of the Princess of Wales exercising in a gym (and the *Daily Mirror* re-published them the following day), there was a considerable outcry. The PCC condemned the two newspapers, and MGN withdrew from the commission. The papers were forced to back down, however. MGN rejoined the PCC, and David Banks, editor of the *Daily Mirror*, later admitted that publishing the photographs, for which the papers had paid a reported £125,000, had been a mistake.

For the most part public debate concentrated on invasions of privacy. Yet journalists faced many more issues than this. The NUJ's ethics council dealt chiefly, until its effective suspension in 1992, with complaints of misrepresentation, especially in the areas of racism, sexism and homophobia. (The union produced guidelines for journalists in these areas – see Figures 12.3 and 12.4 at the end of this chapter.) Many complaints concerned comment and opinion columns in which journalists were regarded as indulging in individual prejudices unsupported by any evidence. This kind of writing was permissible under the PCC code of practice. The Labour MP Clive Soley attempted in 1993 to address misrepresentation in his Press Freedom and Responsibility Bill which proposed a statutory Independent Press Authority empowered to force newspapers to print corrections and apologies (Figure 12.5). This whole matter posed an acute dilemma for journalists. The NUJ and many highly respected 'serious' journalists opposed Soley's proposals on the grounds that they would inhibit press freedom. Some saw a possible trade-off in the Right to Know Bill of another Labour MP, Mark Fisher. Much of the concern behind both measures was the right of 'ordinary people' to fair representation and access to information. A number of victims of 'unfair treatment at the hand of the press and media' formed the pressure group PressWise to campaign for

> 'a rational, balanced and powerful press with a complaints procedure that is respected by all . . . a press which both recognises and demonstrates respect for individual rights . . . a press unafraid of being open and fair.'

In the end both the Soley and Fisher bills fell, and the government's own commitment to more open government was at best half-hearted.

ETHICS

The Daily Error

Newspaper readers deserve a better deal

'GET IT RIGHT' SAYS MP

LABOUR MP Clive Soley is campaigning for readers to be guaranteed corrections when newspapers publish inaccurate information.

His Freedom and Responsibility of the Press Bill will receive its Second Reading on 29 January 1993.

FULL DETAILS INSIDE

"The public rely on news-papers for detailed information. If we cannot trust the Press to get it right, our ability to participate in the democratic process is hampered," he says.

"Misleading headlines and inaccurate reporting are examples of poor journalism. The public deserve better standards.

"The reputation of journalists is at an all-time low, and that is bad for democracy," he says.

"If they are to be the guardians of the public interest, we must be able to trust them.

"Too often innocent people's lives are ruined by the search for sensational stories to sell newspapers," says Clive.

"My Bill is designed to improve journalistic standards and defend Press freedom.

"Accuracy is not too high a price to pay for the Press to win back the trust of its readers."

Press Freedom - a vital public service

Clive Soley's Bill proposes the creation of an Independent Press Authority to monitor threats to Press Freedom, as well as defending the public's right to accuracy in news reporting.

The IPA would report to Parliament every year, and make recommendations to enhance journalists' ability to carry out their jobs.

It would be able to look into ownership and control of Britain's local and national newspapers, the distribution system that discriminates against small circulation publications, and the training of journalists.

"Journalistic ethics play too small a part in the training process," he says. "It might make all the difference if journalists were more conscious of the responsibilities they bear."

'What we need is a tenacious guard dog not a toothless watchdog'

Figure 12.5: The campaign on behalf of Clive Soley's Press Freedom and Responsibility Bill.
Source: Campaign for Press and Broadcasting Freedom

In 1992 the prime minister John Major had undertaken to 'sweep away many of the cobwebs of secrecy'. The white paper arising from this, called *Open Government*, proposed only two relatively minor changes, allowing greater access to a limited range of official information. The D-notice system, by which editors are guided on the reporting of matters considered to be sensitive on national security grounds, was reformed, but not abolished as some journalists had demanded. In fact, throughout the 1980s the government imposed more, rather than fewer, constraints on journalists. The Official Secrets Act, which many felt was in need of a complete overhaul, was reviewed in 1989 but in some respects strengthened. Reporting restrictions in court cases (mentioned above) were refined in 1980, 1981 and 1988. The Police and Criminal Evidence Act, 1984, gave police the right to seek orders forcing journalists to hand over unpublished material, including photographs.

In 1988 the government introduced a ban on broadcasting the voices of people either belonging to, or espousing the views of, designated prohibited organisations, and designed to deny those advocating violence in Ireland access to television and radio air-time. Ministers also exerted pressure on broadcasters in more informal ways: instances included the Death on the Rock incident (see Chapter 11), the Real Lives case when the BBC governors were pressured by the Home Secretary, Leon Brittan, to cancel a programme featuring two Northern Irish politicians, and coverage of the American bombing of Libya in 1987 when the Conservative Party chairman, Norman Tebbit, claimed to have proved the BBC's bias against the US and its military action.

In many respects the restrictions on journalists increased, even though the excesses of journalism were largely unabated. The police, prosecutors and the public seemed more inclined to use the powers available to them, and the courts appeared more receptive to their cases. Photographers were arrested (and in at least one case handcuffed) while 'staking out' a story. The journalist Duncan Campbell's home was raided and documents were seized by police investigating the making of a series of television reports in the so-called Zircon Affair. The number of libel actions increased during the 1980s, and the level of settlements awarded by juries against journalists and the media rose significantly. A relatively new practice emerged of gagging journalists by suing or threatening to sue third parties, such as printers and distributors. These defendants were able to pass any costs back to the media, which would then have to pay for cases they had not been able to defend. It was a tactic much used by the media owner Robert Maxwell to prevent publication of stories about his business activities. In 1993 John Major 'set the seal of approval on . . . a somewhat disreputable practice', according to Steve Platt, editor of *New Statesman*, when he sued the magazine's printers, distributors and major retailers as well as the paper itself for an alleged libel. Platt argued more generally,

> 'English libel law is almost uniquely draconian in the democratic world . . . libel actions have provided a crude means by which the press can be punished.'
>
> *British Editor* (23 May 1993)

Moreover, as libel cases did not qualify for legal aid, suing was largely the perogative of the rich. Many people without access to the often hundreds of thousands of pounds necessary to proceed with a libel action had no recourse other than to accept the situation – even if they had been outrageously defamed by the press.

As the 1980s progressed the situation seemed to get more confused: greater licence was accompanied by more restrictions, public outrage at prurient journalism by increased sales, 'open government' by increased amounts of secrecy, and exposure of the misdeeds of the powerful by fear of the threat of litigation open only to the wealthy. The very concepts of privacy, secrecy, censorship, and taste were notoriously difficult to define with any precision. That applied, too, to the journalist's standard defence for any action, 'public interest', which was central to the PCC code of practice. To many editors 'public interest' simply meant whatever interested the public.

Underlying all this were commercial pressures. In addition to the drive to maintain or improve circulations, magazines in particular were keen to increase advertising revenue. From around 1990 there was what the publisher National Magazines called an explosion of advertorials, advertisements in the form of editorial copy, usually written by staff journalists and implying editorial endorsement. In March 1993 the Periodical Publishers' Association issued guidelines on handling advertorials (see Figure 12.6 at the end of this chapter). These argued that readers should not be misled into thinking that advertorials were part of the editorial content of the magazine, and that staff journalists' by-lines should not appear in them. Traditionally dismissed by journalists as 'misleading puffery', as Nat Mags admitted, advertorials began taking up more and more journalists' time. Their promotion by magazine managers as a useful way of generating income added to the pressures on journalists to favour advertisers and other promoters of goods and services. Many magazines and smaller newspapers relied increasingly on facilities (sometimes known as 'freebies'), ranging from cosmetic samples to trips overseas, to generate copy. In such circumstances journalists complained that it was impossible at least to appear to be fair and accurate. (The practice of accepting facilities was forbidden by some companies, including *The Independent*.)

By the mid-1980s journalists were beset by pressures emanating from employers, advertisers and authority. How were they to deal with them, especially given the decline of the NUJ? The union acknowledged that many journalists had cheerfully embraced the 'tabloid culture', and viewed any restrictions as limiting press freedom. Nevertheless, it became more commonplace to argue, with Raymond Snoddy, the presenter of the Channel 4 series Hard News which looked critically at press misdemeanours, that

> '. . . all journalists, broadsheet no less than tabloid, have got to make the time to get off the treadmill of deadlines to think a little more about what they do, the effect it can have on their fellow citizens and the impact their work is having on the reputation of the press.'
>
> *The Good, the Bad and the Unacceptable*
> (London, 1993)

There was more interest in journalistic ethics in America. The first book devoted to ethical issues in British journalism appeared in 1992, however, and in April 1994 the NUJ organised a conference on ethics which attracted more than 100 participants. Moreover, ethics had also emerged as an issue in a number of professions and occupations, and in business and management. Among those urging more training in ethics was the banking ombudsman Laurence Shurman. From 1990 ethics began to feature more prominently in university journalism courses.

A chief argument was that commercialism should not be allowed to override fundamental standards of integrity. In America, *UK Press Gazette* reported in May 1992, many journalists were concerned that the traditional view of the role of the press of comforting the afflicted and afflicting the comfortable was being subverted, and turned on its head as newspapers tried to improve their circulations and increase their advertising income. The British journalist Paul Foot argued that being a journalist involved making 'dreadful sacrifices of reason, principle and humour' (*Guardian*, 11 April 1994). A trainee journalist noted that his introduction to journalism had led him to believe that to be successful he would have to abandon his 'conscience'.

The alternative, American model did not appear attractive, however. Here the view was that ethics did not simply derive from journalists' almost intuitive news sense. As a result, American journalists divided themselves clearly into 'tabloid' and 'mainstream' categories. The former, who were hardly regarded as journalists at all (see Chapter 2), pursued the stories for which there seemed to be a market: the others adhered to established notions of 'balanced' reporting. One result, it was argued, was that mainstream American journalists imposed limits on their own investigative capabilities, and bored their audiences. David Thomas, an English journalist, noted

> 'Though it might seem absurd to complain that American reporters are obsessed with accuracy and balance, the wood of a good story can often be lost among the trees of journalistic ethics . . . In short, we regard American journalists as dullards who have sacrificed daring and wit for an excessive obsession with accuracy and a willingness to accept whatever pap is fed to them by spokesmen and spin doctors.'
> *Mail on Sunday* (20 February 1994)

Nevertheless, the 'tabloiding' of British journalism signalled fundamental changes in journalism practice. Newspapers, the editor of *The Journal*, an award-winning daily in Newcastle which adopted the tabloid format in 1992, were fast-moving consumer goods no different from Mars Bars which, he admitted, 'may cut to the very quick' for journalists.

A survey by the European Journalism Training Association published in 1994 identified only two concerns common to journalists throughout the European Union: the commitment to 'the truth', and the central need for access to information. Yet the greater public demand, at least in Britain, seemed to be for palatable information and entertainment rather than more difficult 'real' journalism. An opinion poll conducted for the *Observer* in April 1994 found that almost four in ten people believed that the government should censor news and facts in the national interest. Seventy per cent felt that an independent body should decide which facts ought to be kept out of the media. The gulf between journalism orthodoxy and public expectations appeared to be widening.

John Tusa, the managing director of the BBC World Service, suggested that the entire process of journalism should be more open to public scrutiny: '. . . a good journalist,' he wrote, 'is one who shares with the audience the processes, the doubts, the uncertainties, the excitements of the activity which leads to the ultimate choice of words and images put before the audience' (*British Journalism Review*, 1992). One answer was to establish what the *Review* identified in 1989 as

> 'a fundamental credo set in stone which inspires the newcomer [to journalism] towards serving his or her fellow citizens with the facts of life, straight, true, with decency, and even amusement.'

Defining that *credo* was likely to prove difficult. This was true even in broadcasting, where journalists were under a statutory duty to provide balanced reporting. In addition BBC journalists worked to lengthy and in places dense 'Producers' Guidelines', which were intended to establish an ethical framework. In 1989 the Broadcasting Standards Council added a code of practice of its own (revised in 1994), dealing principally with violence, sex, taste and decency, and covering news and current affairs. The 1990 Broadcasting Act required both the ITC and the Radio Authority to produce programme codes, and it established the Broadcasting Complaints Commission. In December 1994, the BBC's Programme Complaints Unit published its first adjudications: news and current affairs accounted for 28 per cent of complaints. Many broadcast journalists themselves complained of over-regulation which was in sharp contrast to the voluntary 'self-restraint' expected of the press.

In 1992 the Association of European Journalists began drawing up a charter for journalism based on separating 'the function of journalism from the business of the media'. The debate over whether journalism was a service or a commodity was a central feature of concerns about journalistic ethics.

Figure 12.1: The NUJ Code of Conduct.
Source: National Union of Journalists

NUJ CODE OF CONDUCT

1. A journalist has a duty to maintain the highest professional and ethical standards.
2. A journalist shall at all times defend the principle of the freedom of the Press and other media in relation to the collection of information and the expression of comment and criticism. He/she shall strive to eliminate distortion, news suppression and censorship.
3. A journalist shall strive to ensure that the information he/she disseminates is fair and accurate, avoid the expression of comment and conjecture as established fact and falsification by distortion, selection or misrepresentation.
4. A journalist shall rectify promptly any harmful inaccuracies, ensure that correction and apologies receive due prominence and afford the right of reply to persons criticised when the issue is of sufficient importance.
5. A journalist shall obtain information, photographs and illustrations only by straightforward means. The use of other means can be justified only by over-riding considerations of the public interest. The journalist is entitled to exercise a personal conscientious objection to the use of such means.
6. Subject to the justification by over-riding considerations of the public interest, a journalist shall do nothing which entails intrusion into private grief and distress.
7. A journalist shall protect confidential sources of information.
8. A journalist shall not accept bribes nor shall he/she allow other inducements to influence the performance of his/her professional duties.
9. A journalist shall not lend himself/herself to the distortion or suppression of the truth because of advertising or other considerations.
10. A journalist shall only mention a person's age, race, colour, creed, illegitimacy, disability, marital status (or lack of it), gender or sexual orientation if this information is strictly relevant. A journalist shall neither originate nor process material which encourages discrimination, ridicule, prejudice or hatred on any of the above-mentioned grounds.

11. A journalist shall not take private advantage of information gained in the course of his/her duties, before the information is public knowledge.
12. A journalist shall not by way of statement, voice or appearance endorse by advertisement any commercial product or service save for the promotion of his/her own work or of the medium by which he/she is employed.

ETHICS

Figure 12.2: Code of Practice.
Source: PCC Press Standards Board of Finance

CODE OF PRACTICE

The Press Complaints Commission is charged with enforcing the following Code of Practice which was framed by the newspaper and periodical industry and ratified by the Press Complaints Commission in April 1994.

All members of the press have a duty to maintain the highest professional and ethical standards. In doing so, they should have regard to the provisions of this Code of Practice and to safeguarding the public's right to know.

Editors are responsible for the actions of journalists employed by their publications. They should also satisfy themselves as far as possible that material accepted from non-staff members was obtained in accordance with this Code.

While recognising that this involves a substantial element of self-restraint by editors and journalists, it is designed to be acceptable in the context of a system of self-regulation. The Code applies in the spirit as well as in the letter.

It is the responsibility of editors to co-operate as swiftly as possible in PCC enquiries.

Any publication which is criticised by the PCC under one of the following clauses is duty bound to print the adjudication which follows in full and with due prominence.

1. **Accuracy**
i) Newspapers and periodicals should take care not to publish inaccurate, misleading or distorted material.
ii) Whenever it is recognised that a significant inaccuracy, misleading statement or distorted report has been published, it should be corrected promptly and with due prominence.
iii) An apology should be published whenever appropriate.
iv) A newspaper or periodical should always report fairly and accurately the outcome of an action for defamation to which it has been a party.

2. **Opportunity to reply**
   A fair opportunity for reply to inaccuracies should be given to individuals or organisations when reasonably called for.

3. **Comment, conjecture and fact**
   Newspapers, whilst free to be partisan, should distinguish clearly between comment, conjecture and fact.

4. **Privacy**
   Intrusions and enquiries into an individual's private life without his or her consent including the use of long-lens photography to take pictures of people on private property without their consent are not generally acceptable and publication can only be justified when in the public interest.

Note – Private property is defined as any private residence, together with its garden and outbuildings, but excluding any adjacent fields or parkland. In addition, hotel bedrooms (but not other areas in a hotel) and those parts of a hospital or nursing home where patients are treated or accommodated.

5. **Listening devices**
   Unless justified by public interest, journalists should not obtain or publish material obtained by using clandestine listening devices or by intercepting private telephone conversations.

6. **Hospitals**
   i) Journalists or photographers making enquiries at hospitals or similar institutions should identify themselves to a responsible executive and obtain permission before entering non-public areas.
   ii) The restrictions on intruding into privacy are particularly relevant to enquiries about individuals in hospitals or similar institutions.

7. **Misrepresentation**
   i) Journalists should not generally obtain or seek to obtain information or pictures through misrepresentation or subterfuge.
   ii) Unless in the public interest, documents or photographs should be removed only with the express consent of the owner.

ETHICS

iii) Subterfuge can be justified only in the public interest and only when material cannot be obtained by any other means.

8. Harassment
i) Journalists should neither obtain nor seek to obtain information or pictures through intimidation or harassment.
ii) Unless their enquiries are in the public interest, journalists should not photograph individuals on private property (as defined in the note to Clause 4) without their consent; should not persist in telephoning or questioning individuals after having been asked to desist; should not remain on their property after having been asked to leave and should not follow them.
iii) It is the responsibility of editors to ensure that these requirements are carried out.

9. Payment for articles
Payment or offers of payment for stories, pictures or information, should not be made directly or through agents to witnesses or potential witnesses in current criminal proceedings or to people engaged in crime or to their associates – which includes family, friends, neighbours and colleagues – except where the material concerned ought to be published in the public interest and the payment is necessary for this to be done.

10. Intrusion into grief or shock
In cases involving personal grief or shock, enquiries should be carried out and approaches made with sympathy and discretion.

11. Innocent relatives and friends
Unless it is contrary to the public's right to know, the press should generally avoid identifying relatives or friends of persons convicted or accused of crime.

12. Interviewing or photographing children
i) Journalists should not normally interview or photograph children under the age of 16 on subjects involving the personal welfare of the child, in the absence of or without the consent of a parent or other adult who is responsible for the children.

ii) Children should not be approached or photographed while at school without the permission of the school authorities.

13. Children in sex cases

1. The press should not, even where the law does not prohibit it, identify children under the age of 16 who are involved in cases concerning sexual offences, whether as victims or as witnesses or defendants.
2. In any press report of a case involving a sexual offence against a child –
   i) The adult should be identified.
   ii) The term 'incest' where applicable should not be used.
   iii) The offence should be described as 'serious offences against young children' or similar appropriate wording.
   iv) The child should not be identified.
   v) Care should be taken that nothing in the report implies the relationship between the accused and the child.

14. Victims of crime

The press should not identify victims of sexual assault or publish material likely to contribute to such identification unless, by law, they are free to do so.

15. Discrimination

i) The press should avoid prejudicial or pejorative reference to a person's race, colour, religion, sex or sexual orientation or to any physical or mental illness or handicap.
ii) It should avoid publishing details of a person's race, colour, religion, sex or sexual orientation, unless these are directly relevant to the story.

16. Financial journalism

i) Even where the law does not prohibit it, journalists should not use for their own profit, financial information they receive in advance of its general publication, nor should they pass such information to others.
ii) They should not write about shares or securities in whose performance they know that they or their close families have a significant financial interest, without disclosing the interest to the editor or financial editor.

iii) They should not buy or sell, either directly or through nominees or agents, shares or securities about which they have written recently or about which they intend to write in the near future.

17. Confidential sources
Journalists have a moral obligation to protect confidential sources of information.

18. The public interest
Clause 4, 5, 7, 8 and 9 create exceptions which may be covered by invoking the public interest. For the purpose of this code that is most easily defined as:

i) Detecting or exposing crime or a serious misdemeanour.
ii) Protecting public health and safety.
iii) Preventing the public from being misled by some statement or action of an individual or organisation.

In any cases raising issues beyond these three definitions the Press Complaints Commission will require a full explanation by the editor of the publication involved, seeking to demonstrate how the public interest was served.

Figure 12.3: NUJ Statement on Race Reporting.
Source: National Union of Journalists

GUIDELINES ON RACE REPORTING

The National Union of Journalists has ratified guidelines for all its members to follow when dealing with race relations subjects. If you are a member these are your guidelines.

RACE REPORTING

- Only mention someone's race if it is strictly relevant. Check to make sure you have it right. Would you mention race if the person was white?
- Do not sensationalise race relations issues, it harms black people and it could harm you.
- Think carefully about the words you use. Words which were once in common usage are now considered offensive, e.g. half-caste and coloured. Use mixed-race and black instead. Black can cover people of Arab, Asian, Chinese and African origin. Ask people how they define themselves.
- Immigrant is often used as a term of abuse. Do not use it unless the person really is an immigrant. Most black people in Britain were born here and most immigrants are white.
- Do not make assumptions about a person's cultural background – whether it is their name or religious detail. Ask them or where it is not possible check with the local race equality council.
- Investigate the treatment of black people in education, health, employment and housing. Do not forget travellers and gypsies. Cover their lives and concerns. Seek the views of their representatives.
- Remember that black communities are culturally diverse. Get a full and correct view from representative organisations.
- Press for equal opportunities for employment of black staff.
- Be wary of disinformation. Just because a source is traditional does not mean it is accurate.

REPORTING RACIST ORGANISATIONS

- When interviewing representatives of racist organisations or reporting meetings or statements or claims, journalists should carefully check all reports for accuracy and seek rebutting or

ETHICS

opposing comments. The anti-social nature of such views should be exposed.
- Do not sensationalise by reports, photographs, film or presentation the activities of racist organisations.
- Seek to publish or broadcast material exposing the myths and lies of racist organisations and their anti-social behaviour.
- Do not allow the letters column or 'phone-in' programmes to be used to spread racial hatred in whatever guise.

STATEMENT ON RACE REPORTING

1. The NUJ believes that the development of racist attitudes and the growth of fascist parties pose a threat to democracy, the right of trade union organisations, a free press and the development of social harmony and well-being.
2. The NUJ believes that its members cannot avoid a measure of responsibility in fighting the evil of racism as expressed through the mass media.
3. The NUJ reaffirms its total opposition to censorship but equally reaffirms the belief that press freedom must be conditioned by responsibility and an acknowledgement by all media workers of the need not to allow press freedom to be abused to slander a section of the community or to promote the evil of racism.
4. The NUJ believes that the methods and the lies of the racists should be publicly and vigorously exposed.
5. The NUJ believes that newspapers and magazines should not originate material which encourages discrimination on grounds of race or colour as expressed in the NUJ's Rule Book and Code of Conduct.
6. The NUJ recognises the right of members to withhold their labour on grounds of conscience where employers are providing a platform for racist propaganda.
7. The NUJ believes that editors should ensure that coverage of race stories should be placed in a balanced context.
8. The NUJ will continue to monitor the development of media coverage in this area and give support to members seeking to enforce the above aims.

GUIDELINES ON TRAVELLERS
- Only mention the word gypsy or traveller if strictly relevant and accurate.

- Give balanced reports seeking travellers' views as well as those of others, consulting the local travellers where possible.
- Resist the temptation to sensationalise issues involving travellers, especially in their relations with settled communities over issues such as housing and settlement programmes and schooling.
- Try to give wide coverage to travellers' lives and the problems they face.
- Strive to promote the realisation that the travellers' community is comprised of full citizens of Great Britain and Ireland whose civil rights are seldom adequately vindicated, who often suffer much hurt and damage through misuse by the media and who have a right to have their special contributions to Irish and British life, especially in music and craft work and other cultural activities, properly acknowledged and reported.

ETHICS

Figure 12.4: NUJ Guidelines on Reporting on homosexuality.
Source: National Union of Journalists

Introduction

Most people don't understand homosexuality, although it is estimated that one in ten of the population is gay. The Minorities Research Group was set up in 1963 – the first organisation *of* as well as *for* gay people.

Homosexual relationships between consenting men over 21 were illegal until 1967 when a new law was passed in England and Wales. This was extended to Scotland in 1982 and Northern Ireland in 1983. Ironically, the law does not mention lesbian relationships.

In spite of the changes in the law, people are still sacked for being homosexual, some suffer physical attacks, others are ridiculed by colleagues or neighbours. Gay bookshops are raided and in 1984, particularly in London, police launched orchestrated attacks on the gay community.

The media is responsible for much of the intolerance towards gay people. Newspaper stories and broadcasts help form and reinforce the biased social attitudes that provoke harassment, discrimination and hostility that seems worse now than at any time since the gay witch hunts in the 1950s.

Journalists should remember Clause 10 of the NUJ's Code of Conduct:

> *'Journalists shall only mention a person's race, colour, creed, illegitimacy, marital status (or lack of it), gender or sexual orientation if this information is strictly relevant. A journalist shall neither originate nor process material which encourages discrimination on any of the above-mentioned grounds.'*

The NUJ's Lesbian and Gay Group has drawn up these guidelines to help journalists portray a more sympathetic and accurate picture of gay people in Britain.

Images of Lesbians and Gay Men

Many journalists seems to have a vague and inaccurate picture of the way gay men and lesbians lead their lives. They are rarely presented in a positive or even objective light. Much reporting is confined to blatant 'queer bashing' or innuendo.

Many pejorative words, phrases and expressions are used, although gay people do not refer to each other in this way eg poofta, lessie, queer, pansy, bent. Some descriptions are preceded by others in quotation marks eg 'self-confessed', 'self-admitted', 'peace' women which mislead the reader.

The media continues to reinforce outdated and stereotyped images of women – often representing them solely as wives, mothers, homemakers, passive, sexually submissive and physically weak, servicing the needs of men. Lesbians are constantly misrepresented and maligned as sexual deviants, 'gay girls', witches, manhaters, extreme feminists, dressed in butch boots and boiler suits.

Items like these fail to acknowledge that gay people read newspapers, listen to the radio and watch television too. As equal members of society, lesbians and gay men want to be described in terms that do not belittle, trivialise or demean them; do not encourage discrimination or distortion; do not sensationalise their activities or put them in a criminal light.

Broadcasting and television produce three particular images: either homosexual women and men are omitted entirely from air and viewing times; or they are discussed as 'problems'; or they are ridiculed in one form or another.

Assumptions to avoid

'All gay people – particularly men – are child molesters and perverts'

This is one of the myths the media keeps alive. Lesbians and gay men are attracted to adult lesbians and gay men, not to children. People attracted to children are known as paedophiles and most are attracted to children of the opposite sex.

'Gay people are dangerous if they work with children or young people'

ETHICS

Some people believe that lesbians and gay men with responsibility over children and young people will attempt to convert them. There is no evidence to suggest that this is the case.

'Gay people make unfit parents'

In the area of child custody and the law, lesbian mothers in particular have been vulnerable to vicious press coverage. This means they risk losing their children. In the great majority of cases of separation or divorce, the legal authorities give custody of children to the father, usually because of their outdated and prejudiced attitudes towards lesbians. Yet gay people are just as good parents as any others.

'Gay people, especially men, are sick'

In the Middle Ages gay people were burned at the stake because they were thought to be in league with the devil. And the myth of sickness still remains: that gay people need medical or psychological help to make them 'normal'.

'Gay people are figures of fun'

To be a gay man does not mean feminine; to be a lesbian does not mean butch. The dungaree-wearing lesbian, the limp-wristed shop assistant, the male hairdresser, women in ties and so on are stereotypes created by the popular press and television to raise a laugh. They are also degrading, inaccurate figures of fun.

'Gay people working in the armed forces are a security risk'

So long as homosexuality has to be hidden, gay people working in these areas can be blackmailed and the media exacerbates this situation by its reporting.

'Public funds for gay centres and projects are a scandalous waste of taxes and ratepayers' money'

Gay people pay rates too! They tend not to have children but contribute towards the education budget. They pay for police forces that frequently harass and abuse them.

Please think twice
When reporting court cases, if it is *really* necessary to include the case of the man charged with what is known as 'gross indecency' with another man – an 'offence' which goes quite unremarked if it takes place between two people of the opposite sex. In the gay community these are known as 'victimless crimes'; there is invariably no public complaint; no offence is caused; the police officer, however, sees this as an opportunity to make an easy arrest.

Publication of names and addressed in these cases almost invariably leads to loss of employment, and extreme distress to the people involved and their families.

PLEASE ASK YOURSELF: is the dubious news-value of such an item really worth the risk of your causing such tragedy?

ETHICS

Figure 12.5: PPA guidelines on advertorials.
Source: Periodical Publishers Association

GUIDELINES FOR SPECIAL ADVERTISING OPPORTUNITIES WITHIN MAGAZINES
produced by
PERIODICAL PUBLISHERS ASSOCIATION
in conjunction with
THE BRITISH SOCIETY OF MAGAZINE EDITORS

Research has shown that magazines enjoy a special one-to-one relationship with their readers. It is this special relationship and their more intense readership that gives magazines a unique ability to position, enhance and brand the products and services of their advertisers.

These characteristics and the informative quality of magazines have not only been important in attracting traditional advertising to magazines, but have also been a key factor in the growing demand from advertisers for special advertising sections, more commonly known as 'advertorials', and sponsored editorial. With these special opportunities, the advertiser is able to draw on the credibility that association with a title confers on a produce or service. Advertorials, described as 'the look that fits', enjoy keen readership, performing as they do the special function of providing consumers with in-depth information on products and services.

As this form of promotion develops and becomes more widespread, it is important that guidelines are available to assist publishers and advertisers and to ensure that special advertising opportunities of this kind continue to work for the benefit of readers, advertisers, editors and publishers alike.

The guidelines have been drawn up following consultation with magazine publishers within PPA and with other relevant industry bodies. These have included the Incorporated Society of British Advertisers (ISBA), the Institute of Practitioners in Advertising (IPA), the Newspaper Publishers Association (NPA), the Newspaper Society (NS), the Institute of Public Relations (IPR), the Public Relations Consultants Association (PRCA) and the Advertising Standards Authority/Committee of Advertising Practice (ASA/CAP).

The guidelines should be applied to any material presented in the main body of a magazine and to any supplement or inserted material. Publishers of dedicated or contract magazines produced by a commercial sponsor should also take note of the guidelines.

In the event of concern and complaint, full details should be forwarded to PPA for advice and conciliation.

Special Advertising Sections
The guidelines are designed to cover those sections of a magazine paid for by the advertiser and created in an editorial style associated with the title.

1. All existing industry guidelines and codes of practice governing advertisements shall be deemed to apply to special advertising sections also. Claims must therefore be substantiated.

2. Readers should not be misled into believing that a particular section of a magazine, which in some way has been paid for by an advertiser, forms part of the editorial content of that publication. Through appropriate labelling, readers should be left in no doubt that what they see before them has been paid for by an advertiser.

3. Material of this kind should, therefore, be clearly identified.

    3.1 The words 'advertisement', 'advertising', '**advertisement** promotion' or '**advertisement feature**' should be used to describe special advertising sections. The term 'advertorial' should NOT be used in this context.

    3.2 The labelling should be consistently applied and should be displayed prominently and legibly on each page or spread affected.

    3.3 Staff writers' by-lines should not appear in special advertising sections.

4. The size and number of special advertising sections within a single issue should not be out of balance with the size and nature of the magazine. The credibility of the title should not be compromised through excessive use of special advertising sections.

Sponsored Editorial
This section of the guidelines is designed to cover those instances where an advertiser pays to have a company/product name associated with editorial in a magazine or a supplement to a magazine.

1 **Material of this kind should be clearly identified as being sponsored.**

2 Editors should ensure that the name of the company/product does not assume undue prominence.

3 The content should be subject to the final approval of the editor.

4 Where an advertiser's company/product name is associated with a competition within the editorial of a magazine in consideration of a payment and/or the supply of prizes, the editor should have the final right of approval for the nature of the competition and the content of the material.

5 Where a charge is made by a publisher for the cost of producing an illustration of a company's product, one of the following forms of wording should appear on a relevant page: 'Suppliers have contributed towards the production costs of some of the editorial photographs/material in this issue/on this page'; 'The editorial photographs on this page are courtesy of the suppliers whose products they feature'; 'This journal includes editorial material/photographs provided and paid for by suppliers'.

6 **Where a product name is mentioned in consideration of the supply of visual or written material for a feature, readers should be informed of the source of the material eg 'photographs/copy supplied by . . .'**

Co-publishing
This section of the guidelines is designed to cover those instances where an advertiser and a publisher have entered into an agreement whereby the advertiser purchases the space to publish a pre-determined number of articles over a number of issues of a particular title.

Although such material contains no overt advertising message, nonetheless it is clearly sponsored and should therefore be subject to the conditions which pertain to sponsored editorial.

13

— GETTING STARTED —

In the early 1990s more than half those graduating in arts subjects from universities in the United Kingdom had ambitions to work in the media. A significant proportion wanted to be journalists. Although the opportunities for entering journalism had widened, the competition for jobs, for training and for places on courses did not decrease. The chance of being admitted to the most popular postgraduate newspaper journalism courses was no greater than about one in 30, and of securing a traineeship with a national newspaper very much less. Almost no vacancies for trainee journalists were advertised: editors could pick and choose from large numbers of high quality candidates whose speculative letters of application were kept on file. Potential recruits were sometimes expected to undertake one or two weeks of unpaid work experience before their names were even added to the list of applicants to be seriously considered. One graduate, who was interviewed and then completed her work experience, waited two years before being shortlisted for a traineeship. At the other end of the scale, a student, partway through a postgraduate journalism course, heard from friends that a national newspaper was looking for a writer, telephoned to express his interest and was interviewed and appointed – all within a week. The attempt to systemise journalism training under the NCTJ appeared to have been only a temporary phenomenon. The kind of pot luck arrangements that had existed in the 1950s had returned.

The fact that in practice there were many ways into journalism was underlined by the introduction of NVQs in the 1990s. This also further fragmented the training system which, since 1952, had pivoted around the NCTJ's national scheme. The idea of more or less unified journalism training, which incorporated reporting, sub-editing, feature writing, newspaper, freelance and magazine journalism, and even photography, was superseded by separate NVQs. In newspaper journalism there were awards in writing; production, and press photography. In magazine journalism, there were five NVQs – in design; subbing; subbing with layout; writing features, and writing news. NVQs were being developed to cover those working in journals, and it was expected that radio journalism would also have a scheme. In publishing, there were seven awards, including those in commissioning; editing; editorial management, and promotion and publicity. While NVQs offered essentially workplace-based training, the provision of courses by universities, colleges, company training schemes, and private training establishments away from the workplace had expanded rapidly. Many were accredited by the NCTJ, the NCTBJ and PTC, and were subject to inspection and evaluation by these bodies. These courses were chiefly dedicated exclusively to journalism and were highly vocational. Others were elements within more general (often media) courses, and were largely practice-based, providing introductions to journalism.

In the 1980s in particular there was a boom in media courses of all types. Journalism courses began to flourish in the 1990s. In 1989 undergraduate courses in media and related studies relevant to journalism were identified at 17 universities in the United Kingdom. By 1994 at least that number of institutions could properly be said to be specialising in some way in journalism at either undergraduate or postgraduate level. Ten universities and colleges were offering undergraduate and postgraduate courses in book publishing alone. There were also courses in public relations (Leeds Business School; Stirling University; Cranfield School of Management; College of St Mark and St John; Bournemouth University), typography and graphic communications (Reading University), and science journalism (Imperial College).

This diversity was enhanced by a growth in the number of private training establishments (see Figure 13.1), and the withdrawal of some of the major provincial publishing companies, including TRN, Westminster Press and EMAP, from the NCTJ system. On the other hand, there was a decline in company provided training in the 1980s, particularly in magazines. Both Reed Business Publishing and Morgan-Grampian abandoned their training schemes. Nevertheless, the qualifications available had expanded over 20 years to include company certificates of achievement, Higher National Diplomas, degrees, Postgraduate Diplomas, and MAs and MScs. There were also City and Guilds media awards, and the Communication Advertising and Marketing Education Foundation (CAM) certificate and diploma, which included media and public relations elements. Large companies, such as Reuters, ITN and the BBC, and individual television stations and newspapers (from 1993,

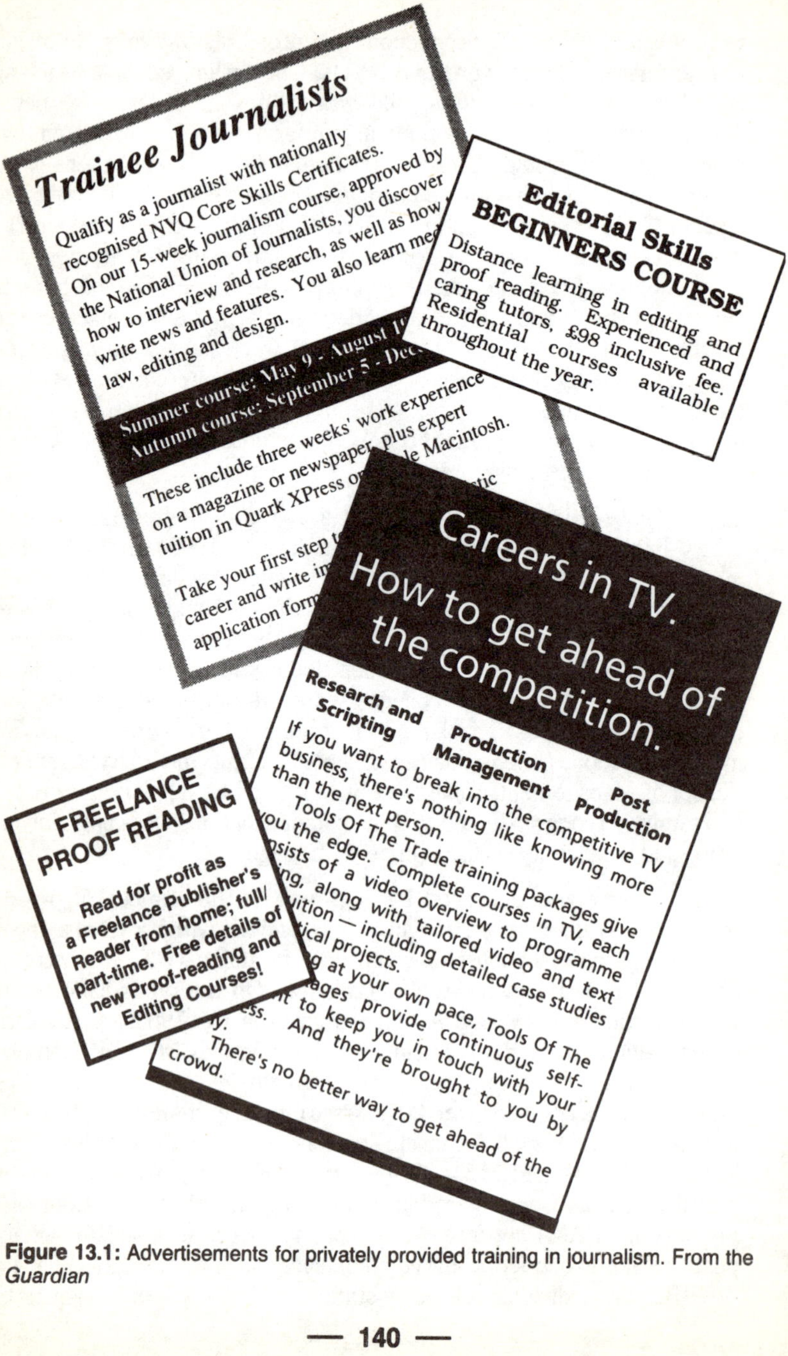

JOURNALISM

Figure 13.1: Advertisements for privately provided training in journalism. From the *Guardian*

including the *Daily Express* and *Daily Mirror*) also offered journalism traineeships. Voluntary bodies, such as the Community Radio Association (CRA), and continuing education institutions provided short courses (often evening classes). Moreover, training and courses became more interdependent: universities contracted with newspapers to provide courses, and companies trained journalists for newspapers outside their own organisations. Into the 1990s, however, the NCTJ's National Certificate largely retained its key role in print journalism training. Other awards were not seen as substitutes for the certificate, although many offered partial exemptions.

The NCTJ scheme was founded on an apprenticeship-type training overseen by the Council. Traineeships were offered by employers and included workplace, distance learning and classroom-based training. Trainees, therefore, entered journalism directly, and training was provided as part of their first job. Company schemes worked in the same way, whether they were accredited by the NCTJ or not. The NCTJ offered an alternative, so-called pre-entry scheme, under which would-be journalists studied for a year on a full-time accredited course at one of a number of colleges. A few pre-entry students were sponsored by employers: most simply hoped the course would lead to a job in journalism.

The NCTJ system had been designed principally for people under 24 (there were *ad hoc* arrangements for those aged 24–30, but not much to cover people over 30), either already employed, or with good employment prospects. It tied both employer and trainee to a period of indenture lasting between 18 months and three years. Critics accused the scheme of inflexibility, and of being unadaptable to changing circumstances. Attempts to extend the scheme to include both magazine and radio journalism in the 1970s had failed. Some employers felt that the training was too general: they wanted something more closely tailored to their specific requirements. Many trainees (especially graduates) complained that the period of indenture was unnecessarily long. As newspapers in particular cut back on production staff, they undertook to retrain redundant print workers in journalism: most of them were over 30. The number of other applicants over 30 began to rise. Such people were not really covered by the scheme. The NCTJ had been formed as a response to the observations of the 1949 Report of the Royal Commission on the Press that there was a direct relationship between the low status of journalism and a lack of formal training for journalists. By the 1990s at least eight out of ten (and possibly as many as nine out of ten) people entering journalism underwent some initial formal training. The Book House Training Centre alone offered more than 80 types of courses for people working in publishing. The NCTJ was also possibly a victim of its own success. As the quality of entrants into journalism rose, it was more difficult to match them with the routine of weekly newspaper journalism. As long ago as 1975 the Council recognised, 'It is unlikely that the graduate journalist would find that work on a weekly newspaper would offer sufficient job satisfaction . . .'. The bigger change, however, was economic. Under the NCTJ scheme the costs of training were borne overwhelmingly by employers, and because the training was general, it equipped trainees to get jobs elsewhere once their training was complete. Many left virtually the day their indentures ended. In the 1980s magazines and provincial newspapers in particular saw training as an area where they could maintain their commitment while reducing their costs. Those costs began to be picked up either by the trainees themselves, or other employers.

Training and courses

In the 1990s would-be journalists faced a bewildering choice of routes into journalism. It was still possible to get a job that provided no training at all. Many small weekly newspapers, specialist journals and press offices had untrained staff. The idea of starting as a secretary or editorial assistant, and graduating to journalism had not been totally abandoned. A variation which became more attractive (or, at least, more common) was to take up freelance journalism without having previously worked on the staff of a paper, radio station or television news room. Short courses that addressed the outlines of researching, writing and marketing articles were targeted at such people. Most journalists, however, sought – and most employers provided – some training (as noted above). From 1993 NVQs were more common, although the NCTJ scheme persisted. (The Council also became an NVQ assessing body.) This placed the responsibility on the potential trainee to secure a job first. NCTJ pre-entry courses continued to run at colleges in Harlow, Darlington, Portsmouth, Preston, Sheffield, Cardiff and Belfast, and photographers' courses in Sheffield, but their future was in doubt. The first undergraduate courses appeared at City, Sheffield, Bournemouth and Central Lancashire universities. The number of postgraduate courses, initiated in the 1970s by the University of Wales, Cardiff College, increased, albeit slowly. The latest notable venture was the opening of the Scottish Centre for Journalism Studies at Strathclyde University. Establishments offering private tuition, sometimes with the backing of the NCTJ, discovered an expanding market. Finally, journalism elements appeared in greater and greater numbers in media, communications, literature and other courses in higher education. It soon became impossible to chart a simple route through the maze of what was on offer.

Deciding the best way to start a career in journalism was increasingly a matter of personal choice. Fewer journalists started work before completing a university degree course. Many were introduced to, and even received their first instruction in journalism at university. The idea of getting a postgraduate qualification, equivalent to the American system of attending professional school, became more popular. The majority of first jobs, however, were still to be found in the provincial press, local radio and trade magazines. The magazine sector (as has already been mentioned) expanded considerably in the 1980s. Radio provided another area of expansion, less because of the growth of incremental ILR stations (which tended to have small staffs of journalists), and more as a result of the development by the BBC of Radio 5 (Live) in the 1990s. The national media generally, however, took an increasing proportion of trainees. (There were also new opportunities in satellite television and teletext services.) Those wanting to be journalists were best advised to research thoroughly the opportunities available. Too often, it seemed, applicants were attracted by what they presumed to be the glamour or image of the job without having any clear idea what journalism entailed.

—— Useful sources of information ——

BBC Journalists Training, Broadcasting House, London W1A 1AA
BBC Local Radio Training Unit, Grafton House, 379 Euston Road, London NW1 3AU
Book House Training Centre, 45 East Hill, Wandsworth, London SW18 2QZ
CAM Foundation, Abford House, 15 Wilton Road, London SW1V 1NJ
City and Guilds Regional Advisory Council for Further Education, Tavistock House South, Tavistock Square, London WC1H 9LR
Community Radio Association, 119 Southbank House, Black Prince Road, London SE1 7SJ

Institute of Journalists, Suite 2, Dock Offices, Surrey Quays, Lower Road, London SE16 2YS

Institute of Public Relations, The Old Trading House, 15 Northburgh Street, London EC1V 0PR

National Council for the Training of Broadcast Journalists, 188 Lichfield Court, Sheen Road, Richmond, Surrey TW9 1BB

National Council for the Training of Journalists, Latton Bush Centre, Southern Way, Harlow, Essex CM18 7BL

National Union of Journalists, Acorn House, 314 Gray's Inn Road, London WC1X 8DP

Periodicals Training Council, Imperial House, 15–19 Kingsway, London WC2B 6UN

Publishing Qualifications Board, 344–354 Gray's Inn Road, London WC1X 8BP

Training opportunities

(The list is *not* exhaustive.)

Newspaper journalism

Company training (NCTJ accredited)

Croydon Advertiser Group
Eastern Counties Newspapers
Kent and Sussex Courier
The Midland News Association
Southern Newspapers
* A consortium of newspapers subscribes to courses run by the North East Wales Institute

Company training (outside NCTJ)

Daily Express
Daily Mirror
East Midlands Allied Press
Financial Times
Reuters

Sunday Times
Thomson Regional Newspapers
Times
Westminster Press

NCTJ pre-entry courses

Belfast Institute of Further and Higher Education
Cardiff Institute of Higher Education
University of Central Lancashire
College of Technology, Darlington
College of Commerce, Dublin (Two-year course)
Harlow College
Highbury College, Portsmouth
Stradbroke College, Sheffield
Cornwall College, Redruth

Pre-graduate courses

Napier University, Edinburgh
City College, Norwich
West Surrey College of Art and Design

Undergraduate courses

Bournemouth University
University of Central Lancashire
City University, London
Dublin City University
London College of Printing
Sheffield University
Southampton Institute
University of Teesside

Postgraduate courses

Cardiff Institute of Higher Education
University of Wales, College of Cardiff
University of Central Lancashire
City University, London
Dublin City University
Strathclyde University

Magazine journalism

Company training
EMAP
IPC

Pre-graduate courses
London College of Printing

Postgraduate courses
University of Wales, Cardiff College
City University
London College of Printing

Broadcast journalism

Company training
BBC Local Radio
BBC Television
BBC World Service
ITN

Pre-graduate courses
West Surrey College of Art and Design

Undergraduate courses
Bournemouth University
Nottingham Trent University

Postgraduate courses
University of Wales, Cardiff College
University of Central England
University of Central Lancashire
City University, London

College of Technology, Darlington
Falmouth School of Art and Design
Highbury College, Portsmouth
London College of Printing
University of the West of England
University of Westminster

Voluntary bodies

Birmingham Community Radio Training
Community Radio Association

Photography

NCTJ pre-entry course

Stradbroke College, Sheffield

Postgraduate courses

London College of Printing

Public relations

Company graduate training

Biss Lancaster
The Borodin Management and Communications Group
Burson–Marsteller
Charles Barker Lyons
Daniel J. Edelman
Harvard Public Relations
Paragon Communications
The Rowland Company
Shandwick PR Company

Public sector

Government Information Service

Undergraduate courses

Bournemouth University
Leeds Metropolitan University
College of St Mark and St John, Plymouth

Postgraduate courses

Cranfield School of Management
Stirling University

Book publishing

Undergraduate courses

Middlesex University
London College of Printing

Postgraduate courses

Exeter University
Middlesex University
London College of Printing
Napier University
Oxford Brookes University
Reading University
Stirling University
West London Institute

Opportunities for ethnic minority candidates

BBC (training schemes)
Sunday Times (traineeships)
Vauxhall College, London (access courses in print and broadcast journalism)
Westminster University (one year pre-entry courses in radio and magazine journalism)

14

'WHY I WANT TO BE A JOURNALIST'

> '. . . it is the combination of
> practical experience, acceptance of
> the professional ethos, and the
> acquisition of skill in the training
> process that makes the complete journalist.'
> NCTJ, *Training in Journalism*

The persistent idea that, unlike many professions, journalism essentially has to be learned on the job has placed a premium on experience. Yet that is precisely what the aspiring journalist has been most likely to lack. As the competition for training, places on courses and jobs has increased, so there has been a scramble among candidates to demonstrate their commitment to journalism, and to acquire a modicum of prior experience. A standard method has been to undertake some student journalism. The value of this kind of experience has not been proved conclusively. Many editors have tended simply to dismiss student journalism as irrelevant: some have considered it detrimental. This has been largely because in the United Kingdom, unlike America, student journalism has been so poorly organised that it has not been subject to the same set of disciplines as professional journalism. That is, everyone involved in student journalism (media 'owners', journalists and audience) were drawn from the same narrow population group. Student media in the United Kingdom have not had to sell themselves; student journalism was not a preparation for acquiring what the NCTJ called 'a powerful and virtually instinctive identification with the readership' of popular papers. Many professional journalists have seen student journalism, therefore, as dangerously self-indulgent.

Successful professional journalists who did work in the student media have often claimed, though, that the experience was worthwhile. Apart from allowing them to practise journalism (at whatever level), usually with others who shared both their interests and ambitions, it often led to them making useful contacts with professional journalists. It was also more or less inevitable that, as the number of graduate journalists increased, so a background in student journalism became more common. By the 1990s executives recruiting trainee journalists had themselves often been student journalists. Another considerable advantage of student journalism was that it provided access to up-to-date equipment at a time of rapid technological change. The technology available to student media has often been more advanced than that used by small newspapers, and that available on dedicated journalism courses. Some journalism students and trainees have had more experience with and knowledge of such systems than their prospective employers.

The sometimes jaundiced views expressed by editors and other journalists of student journalism have no doubt encouraged some people looking to acquire prior experience to try to do so while spending the almost obligatory year travelling. This has ranged from work experience on English language newspapers in Eastern Europe, and shadowing television reporters in Scandinavia, to translating articles for magazines in Asia. Again, while often admirable and adventurous in themselves, such activities have been likely to prove little to the editor of a provincial daily newspaper or business-to-business magazine. Indeed, they may have served only to convince an editor of the applicants' underlying desires to be foreign correspondents (an ambition shared by thousands) rather than to spend a year-and-a-half reporting local council meetings, or writing up trade news paragraphs. There has also been some scepticism among journalists over the growing practice of students spending short periods of time travelling around the offices of certain national newspapers and consumer magazines. The kind of work experience offered for the most part has been extremely limited: writing diary paragraphs, researching for feature writers, shadowing, sitting in on a section desk, going on photo-shoots. This rapidly evolved into something of a circus.

Although less glamorous, and possibly less easily arranged, work experience which has demonstrated both a sense of initiative and an awareness of the more mundane bulk of day-to-day journalism has also tended to be much more impressive. Many provincial newspapers, trade magazines, local radio stations, independent production companies and (perhaps more rarely) book publishers, freelance journalism agencies, television stations and public relations companies have been willing to offer work experience. This has tended to be at two levels: the introductory, work shadowing type, and the kind which has allowed the participants to undertake 'live' work under supervision. Some organisations have structured schemes; for example, many provincial papers participate in the Newspapers in Education Scheme (NIES). This has been a way of gaining some initial understanding of newspapers and how they work, and of journalists and journalism. Similar arrangements have been introduced, particularly in consumer magazines, for university students (especially those involved in student journalism). It has normally been taken as a measure of a person's interest in journalism that they have moved on from the first kind of experience to the latter. It has also been important not to confuse the two: one evening newspaper in the north of England has physically divided its NIES students from those on second-level work experience. In most newspapers, however, it has been necessary to make it clear what kind of work experience was being sought.

Despite all these schemes, there has been little to prevent would-be journalists from going it alone. While proper freelancing has never been recommended (although some people have successfully started out this way), establishing oneself as a more casual occasional contributor to newspapers, magazines or broadcasting has provided a great deal of useful experience. It has been of particular relevance to photographers, many of whom move straight into freelance careers at the completion of their training. There can be no doubt that freelancing has usually put tyro journalists on their mettle: they have to accept full responsibility for their work, often without much professional guidance. The advice has usually been to start small and progress slowly.

Freelancing has also been taken to include voluntary work. The types of freelancing undertaken by emerging journalists have commonly included

- submitting photographs of newsworthy events (accidents, etc) to local papers
- filing written reports of sports matches to local radio
- contributing editorially to community projects, such as commemorative booklets
- acting as press officers for voluntary organisations

- writing the copy for leaflets
- researching and writing articles on specialist topics for magazines
- editing a newsletter with a public circulation

All these activities would in some way bring the aspiring journalist into contact with the media.

None of the work experience ideas or schemes mentioned above has really stood alone. Each has complemented the others. One type of experience has often led to another; for example, telephoning the local paper (or radio station) with information, or submitting photographs, has regularly led to invitations to spend some time in the office. Similarly, a period of work experience has encouraged magazines later to commission articles. This kind of developing relationship has been much more possible outside the large national media, and has generally been regarded as indicating a more genuine commitment to journalism as a career. A single article, no matter how impressive in itself, nor how prestigious the publication in which it appeared, could always be discounted as a one-off. The judicious would-be journalist has looked to gain as wide a variety of work experience as possible. Almost everywhere applicants for first jobs in journalism have been asked the standard question, *Why do you want to be a journalist?* The most satisfactory answers have invariably been those which have drawn on a broad knowledge and first-hand understanding acquired during work experience.

The above has applied to photographers. For them, however, there has also been the option of collating a portfolio of unpublished work. Stories which remain unprinted, press releases unreleased, and books unpublished have tended to make little impression: they raised suspicions that there must have been something wrong with them if they were rejected. This applied less to photographs chiefly because photographers needed to demonstrate a level of technical ability not paralleled in written journalism. The NCTJ recognised that there were two components to press photograph: photography and journalism.

Taking off

Being adequately prepared for the interview (and tests) leading to first jobs in journalism has been difficult. Editors themselves have had no fixed ideas of what they are looking for. That became more evident

'WHY I WANT TO BE A JOURNALIST'

during the 1980s, and in 1994 research was started to try to identify just what was sought in the emerging generation of journalists. There have been some clues, however. The NCTJ provided guidelines to interviewing, and formal tests to be put to, applicants. The syllabi of journalism training and education schemes as they have developed over the past 40 years have also indicated what has been expected. At the same time, it must be remembered that, as training has moved away from the NCTJ model, a greater variety of expectations has probably emerged. It has been possible to identify different 'types' which appear to have stood a better chance of successfully applying for jobs in certain organisations. Nevertheless, a common standard seemed to prevail for the most part.

The NCTJ proposed seven questions for editors to ask interviewees:

- Is the applicant too shy or too brash?
- Will the applicant develop into the sort of person who will establish good relations with sources of information amongst the public at large?
- Does the applicant read newspapers, periodicals, and books?
- Does the applicant recognise what would interest the reader?
- Does the applicant have a sufficient grasp of current affairs to be able to understand and interpret the happening she/he will be recording?
- Can the applicant express her/himself clearly in conversation?
- Can the applicant write?

Although that list (amended only to eliminate the original gender bias) was published in the 1970s, it remained relevant nearly 20 years later. The NCTJ pre-entry selection test, which was put to applicants at the time of their interviews, reflected the concerns in the list. Again, two decades later it was common practice to set applicants a test at interview. The elements were broadly the same as those in the NCTJ original. What was being evaluated could be listed briefly under five headings.

Media awareness

Although articulated by the NCTJ as reading, an awareness of all the media has been an essential attribute of journalists. One editor advised would-be journalists, 'Instead of consuming the media, be consumed *by* the media.' The advice has rarely been taken. Aspiring journalists have continued to divide themselves into distinctive and exclusive groups:

those who read only the *Guardian*, *The Independent* and *Observer*, and those only *The Sun*, *Daily Mirror* and *News of the World*; viewers of Newsnight, Panorama and World in Action, and viewers of News at Ten, The Word and Def II; listeners to Today, and to the hourly bulletins on ILR; subscribers to *New Statesman and Society* and *Economist*, and to *Vogue* and *Bella*. These have been less caricatures than accurate reflections of personal taste. The shift the journalist has been expected to make has been from a personal to a professional approach to the media: *everything* needed to be at least looked at.

The standard journalist's consumption of the media consisted of ALL the morning papers; evening and weekly papers where available; Today and ILR news output; Channel 4 News, the BBC Nine o'Clock News, News at Ten and Newsnight; the *New Statesman*, *Spectator*, *Economist*, *Private Eye*. In addition, the news agency copy from PA and Reuters, and a variety of publications and free-sheets would be taken at the office. Then there were the specialist press and programmes which addressed either professional or personal interests. Finally, all journalists read their own papers or magazines, listened to their own programmes, watched their own broadcasts. Few people not being paid to be interested in the media could afford to sustain that level of consumption. Indeed, by the late 1980s it was unlikely that many journalists in the local press or broadcasting, or on magazines still bothered to. There were instances of even quite large regional daily newspaper officers ceasing in the 1980s to take *The Sun* and the *Daily Star*. It was possible to read, listen and view broadly without becoming a full-time media consumer. One way was to vary habits; to buy the media like most other products – by seeing if they were worthwhile. Most people bought newspapers (and to a lesser extent watched television programmes) through force of habit. A journalist was not similarly restricted: *The Sun* might have an interesting exclusive one day, the *Guardian* a fascinating feature article the next. Both radio and television could be taped to be sampled later. It was not always necessary to watch every news and current affairs programme from beginning to end. It was possible to develop a pattern of manageable but comprehensive media consumption.

Current affairs

At a time when most education was finally abandoning the notion of a useful general knowledge, in favour of increased specialisation and better knowledge management, journalism was dedicating itself to it.

Journalists were expected to be generalists in the extreme, capable of turning their hands to any subject at a moment's notice. An NCTJ pre-entry selection test in the mid-1970s contained 11 questions on current affairs. If the specific details were amended, all might have been asked by an editor, or course admissions tutor in 1994. They included:

- Name the holders of the following offices:
    Archbishop of Canterbury
    Attorney General
    Foreign Secretary
    Prime Minister of India
    TUC General Secretary
- What is the present basic salary of a Member of Parliament?
- Who is the General Secretary of UNO?
- When was the last general election?
- When and where will the next Olympics be held?

The NCTJ also ran 'aptitude tests' for applicants, which included questions like 'What do the initials RA stand for?'

By the 1990s the questioning might have been more sophisticated, but the principles were the same. In 1993 applicants interviewed for places on the postgraduate course in newspaper journalism at City University were set questions designed to test their detailed reading of newspapers over the preceding few weeks. The relationship between a knowledge of current affairs and media consumption (noted above) was a close one. Editors of local papers and local radio station managers looked specifically for local knowledge. Some preferred to hire local people for this reason; but increasingly it became apparent that if they recruited more widely they had more and better applicants to choose from. The extent to which a potential recruit from, say, Lancashire, who had been to university in Birmingham and postgraduate journalism school in Cardiff, could demonstrate adequate knowledge of Norwich was seen as acting as an additional test of journalistic aptitude. The key was not only to conduct some basic research – get information from the local tourist office, council, chamber of commerce – but to *read the local papers* and particularly the one offering the job. (The task was slightly more difficult with local radio, but tapes were obtainable.) National media organisations also expected an awareness of a wide range of topics based on an understanding of their position in the market, the interests of their audiences, and their individual approaches.

'Flair'

Throughout the 1970s and into the 1980s many journalists retained a deep suspicion of graduate trainees. They were believed, as the NCTJ noted (see above), not to share the interests of the mass of readers and listeners, and to be uninterested in the minutiae which made up much routine journalism. Graduates, it was argued, might have the ability to learn what passed for 'news sense', but they did not have 'an instinctive news sense' (NCTJ). Graduates did not know 'what made ordinary people tick'. This attitude undoubtedly arose out of the elitism of British higher education which until the 1990s admitted no more than 15 per cent of the school population. From the 1950s journalism training in the United Kingdom became increasingly divorced from that in almost every other country in the world. Supported by UNESCO and led by the example of America, journalism training elsewhere was based on undergraduate courses and professional schools in universities and colleges. This approach was often denigrated in the United Kingdom as being 'too theoretical'. In fact, the UK system satisfied the needs of the media industries in providing training only to those already in employment. Fundamental changes in the provision of education – by the early 1990s the government's target was for at least 30 per cent of school-leavers to be in higher education – and in employment patterns (discussed earlier) made it much less likely that applicants for first jobs were either non-graduates or entirely new to journalism.

Techniques for discerning 'news sense' in potential journalists, therefore, arguably increased in importance – at least in the minds of editors. Two types of test were typically set: the news agenda (or bulletin) and the news story. In the former, applicants were asked to put in order of priority for either that day's paper or news bulletin a number of news stories from a list. In the latter, they would be asked to write a news story from material provided. The exercise would most likely be closely related to the practices of the specific paper, magazine or broadcast organisation. What was being asked was not only, 'Can you recognise news?', but also 'Can you recognise what is news for this paper (magazine, radio or television station)?' Editors would be looking for an awareness not only of what might be termed 'raw' news values, but also many of the debates raised earlier, such as the balance between 'good' and 'bad' and 'important' and 'interesting' news, and how they were reflected in their own papers or broadcasts.

Lists of news items dated rapidly, and were of little practical use subsequently. One in the spring of 1994 might have included the following:

1. Prime Minister in new row with Euro-sceptics
2. Korean stand-off reaches 'danger point', say Americans
3. County education committee makes £3 million cuts
4. Town centre closed by fire. Two shops burnt out
5. Local non-league football team reaches FA Cup fifth round for first time
6. Regional branch of Greenpeace claims government is failing to meet Earth Summit commitments
7. Largest employer in town lays off 500 workers
8. Plans for new hypermarket on former factory site on edge of town to be unveiled today
9. Princess of Wales reveals new 'friendship'
10. Cut in interest rates likely

The task would have been to list four or five items, in order, for a midday local radio news bulletin, or the front page of a local evening newspaper. The final choice would depend on the news values of the radio station or newspaper. The items on this list would have been very different if the test had been set by the BBC, or Reuters.

Similarly, news story tests set by the *Times* or a news agency specialising in financial reporting would have borne little resemblance to the ones used by a local newspaper. Moreover, as more journalists came to be recruited for their specialist knowledge (see Chapter 2), a news test made less sense than close questioning on the specific topic. Nevertheless, the news writing test (whether general or specialist) remained common. Some editors expected applicants to do no more than write an introduction to a story, based on a relatively small amount of written material; some asked for stories of between 150 and 250 words; others set a short exercise like this one:

> Write a paragraph from the following details:
>
> Accident on Monday morning at 9 a.m. at the junction of Straight Street and Albany Road, Anytown.

A coach crashed into the back of the trailer of a lorry belonging to Hercules and Co., haulage contractors of Anytown. The driver was Mr Antony Allan who lives in Wellesley Crescent, Popleton.

The coach was driven by Gerald Johnston of 42 Harold Road, Anytown. Owned by Anytown Coaches.

Coach was taking a party of 20 schoolgirls from the Croxbourne School, Anytown on a day's outing to a nature reserve at Broadstead. They suffered from shock.

Everyone taken to St Agnes Hospital, Anytown, by a fleet of ambulances. All were treated but none detained.

Writing

A gross assumption has often been made (with some justification) that beginner journalists cannot write. That is, that they do not have the experience to write in a journalistic fashion. Few journalists have pressured complete beginners to produce ideal stories. All the same, any copy was expected to be written in a style close to that of the hiring paper, magazine or broadcasting organisation. Again, the key was to be familiar with the specific publication or programme.

A standard way of beginning to develop an awareness of journalistic styles of writing has been to take stories from one kind of paper or magazine or news bulletin and re-write them in the style of another. The basics of news story writing have always been quite simple. The three component parts have been identified as:

- the 'angle' or 'line', sometimes called the 'news peg'. This is what the writer has decided is the most important or most interesting aspect of the story
- the 'intro' (introduction), the opening paragraph containing the essence of the 'angle' in preferably a short single sentence
- the story structure, moving from the broad outline of the angle in the introduction to more specific detail, in priority order.

Harold Evans, a former editor of both *The Times* and *The Sunday Times*, thought that the ideal intro was 30–40 words long. Leslie Sellers, a former production editor of the *Daily Mail*, produced a check-list of six items to ensure that every story got '10 out of 10':

1. Are the facts right?
2. Are there any loose ends?
3. Is everything clear?
4. Does it flow like honey? . . . The sequence should be perfect, the facts blindingly simple.
5. Does it make any unnecessary demands on the customer?
6. Can it be simplified?

The Simple Subs Book
(Pergamon Press, 1968)

While the execution has differed from medium to medium, the principles applied to all journalism – including press releases, book jacket blurbs, and picture captions.

Many journalists have struggled for years to get Sellers' 10 out of 10 on their stories. The most that has been held out for beginners is that they have tried. What has made even the most diffident writing at least look more acceptable has been the correct presentation. Again, the principles of copy presentation, founded on newspaper practice, have been generally accepted by all the media. In radio since the 1980s there has been less inclination to insist on formal copy formatting, or on cue sheets to accompany tape. Nevertheless, presenting copy 'properly' has retained the advantages of appearing more professional and being less likely to misinterpretation.

Most 'hard' copy (on paper), including picture captions, feature articles for magazines and stories for radio and television, have been perfectly acceptable in this kind of format. The same has become true, with minor adjustments, for copy submitted electronically, either on disk or transmitted by modem (see Figure 14.1).

Bromley/London   24.03.94   Sample/1

The way to lay out copy is with headers which clearly identify

the author (top left), the date (centre) and the story (right).

More

Sample/2

You may be asked to place the information in a different order, or to include other material. If you are not known to the news room, you ought to include your address and telephone number.

The word 'sample' is what is called a 'catchline' or 'slug'. It should be short, relevant to the story and specific.

Generic catchline words, such as 'fire', 'crash' and 'death', are likely to appear on dozens of different stories unless avoided altogether.

Never use obscenities for catchlines. Nor words which are also used as instructions in journalism. 'Kill' means 'scrap this story'. 'Dead' means it has already been scrapped. Do not try to be funny in catchlines.

The number (extreme right) is the 'folio number' and identifies the pages of the copy and their sequence.

A considerable amount of space should be left between the headers and the start of the story itself. If there is a photograph to go with the story, you should indicate that in this space by typing in 'With pic'.

More

Sample/3

The story should be double-spaced, with wide margins left and right. An extra line should be left between paragraphs.

Keep the paragraphs short. They can always be linked together later.

Type on only one side of the paper. Do not break up a paragraph at the end of a page. Only begin typing on a new page after completing the previous paragraph.

Do not worry about the apparent waste of paper. Many of the conventions of copy presentation derive from the days of hot metal production.

Lots of space was left for sub-editors to make corrections and changes and add setting instructions.

Although this is no longer strictly necessary, journalists are used to receiving copy in this kind of format. To them it looks more 'professional'.

Keep your own corrections to a minimum. Copy should be what is called 'clean' – neatly word processed (or typed) with no pen or pencil marks, or crossings-out.

More

Sample/4

At the end of each page (folio) put 'more' to indicate that other pages follow.

At the end of the last page, put 'END' to show that the story is complete.

END

Figure 14.1: Copy presentation.

English

Nothing has exercised the minds of journalists more consistently in recent years than the state of the English language, its general usage and its role in journalism. A general consensus has emerged that the basics of English language are no longer taught in schools, nor an application of them developed in universities; that literacy levels have fallen, and that it has become impossible to maintain journalistic standards of English. Keith Waterhouse, a columnist in the *Daily Mail* and a respected authority on clear journalistic English, observed

> 'Back in the quaint hot metal era you could not get a job in newspapers without a sound grasp of English, and that included grammar . . . Now grammar's gone to the pictures or more likely down the video arcade.'
>
> *British Journalism Review* (1993)

Editors and journalism tutors have complained about having to instruct young journalists in remedial English.

A 'sound grasp of English' included at least grammar, punctuation and spelling, and tests were devised and revised to encourage good English and discourage the 'sub-literate trainee' (Waterhouse). Points of contention included the proper use of the apostrophe (especially in *it's*), and the littering of copy with commas in almost every place except the correct ones. A pre-entry test in English might ask applicants to define words, such as *complement*; to spell *accommodate*; to provide simpler more effective words for phrases, such as *at the present time*. This test is part of one set at City University in 1994:

Correct the following sentences:

1. All proffesionals need a license to practise.
2. The knife is as sharp – if not sharper than mine.
3. Walking across the road, the car ran him over.
4. Outside the stationary shop was a stationary car.
5. Womens magazines attract both male and female journalists.
6. The criteria for choosing students is performance not promise.

Some newspaper executives worried that declining literacy was being reflected in falling circulations. They suggested that papers should use more illustrations to tap into a 'graphic literacy', especially among the young. Appealing to readers, it appeared, did not necessarily square with being pedantic over half-forgotten syntactical correctness. This was even more obvious in broadcasting where scripts were written in colloquial English, reflecting more closely the way in which English was spoken. Rules were no longer necessarily applicable. Advertising, too, fractured English to make its points. And, it had to be said, newspaper headlines, which Sellers urged should be 'idiomatic', developed their own syntax. A great deal of the use to which English was put in the media was not *telling* but *selling*. It then fed back into common usage. One mistake repeatedly made by beginning journalists has been to try to write in headlines or sound bites. Simplicity, clarity and conciseness have always had the edge.

Over 30 years what has been expected of people hoping to embark on a career in journalism has probably changed very little. In some ways, the applicants have changed more. It has been necessary for many journalists to make adjustments to the increase in the numbers of graduates and those with journalistic skills and experience acquired at college and university wanting to become journalists. The expectations of the newer generation have often been quite different from those of journalists used to NCTJ-directed training. This has continued to stress the established virtues of journalism: learning slowly through accumulated experience; being immersed in the media; developing a broad general knowledge; nurturing a 'news sense'; writing simply and crisply; and using 'good' English. Doubts may have been cast over the 'tell it straight' style of journalism, and a new emphasis on presentation and packaging may have been evolving, but the NCTJ still ranked as the number one aim of its newspaper journalism syllabus, 'To recognise, obtain and select important, relevant and newsworthy facts . . .'

15

RESOURCES

Many people make no attempt to enter journalism because they feel 'it's not for the likes of me'. Others drift into journalism because 'it seemed like a good idea at the time'. Information about journalism is normally hard to find. The best approach is to exercise your journalistic bent and dig out for yourself what you need.

What is journalism?

UK Press Gazette, published weekly on Monday, is the only publication devoted to journalism on regular sale. It covers the major developments in the media from a journalist's point of view, and has sections on newspapers, magazines and broadcasting. It also carries job ads.

'Media *Guardian*' (Monday). This has without doubt the best selection of job ads. The features cover the media, rather than journalism.

There are media pages weekly in the *Times* and *The Independent*.

The *Journalist's Handbook* (quarterly) is free to practising journalists.

Making It: An Insight into the Making of *The Guardian* (1994) is a video produced by the newspaper.

Journalism

Take the advice given earlier and consume masses of it first-hand. Read broadsheet and tabloid newspapers, and a selection of magazines. Listen at least to the Today programme on Radio 4, and to a good ILR news service. Watch one ITV/Channel 4 and one BBC TV news programme. Tape what you can't listen to or watch, and check out later what you missed.

What the papers say – BBC 2, Stop Press – Radio 5 Live, and Medium wave – BBC Radio 4 cover journalism and related issues. Other television and radio programmes come and go.

Collections of journalism can be useful and entertaining. Dated by-lined columns are not the best introduction to journalism, however.

Journalists

Almost any journalist's autobiography or memoirs will provide some (usually highly-coloured) introduction.

Derek Jameson: *Touched by Angels* (1988), and *Last of the Hot Metal Men* (1990).

Wensley Clarkson: *Dog Eat Dog: Confessions of a Tabloid Journalist* (1990) is pretty self-explanatory.

Anne Sebra, *Battling for News: The Rise of the Woman Reporter* (1994) covers a neglected area.

Skills

Being able to use a keyboard gives you a flying start. You should aim for about 40 words per minute. Typing and word processing classes are usually available at most further education colleges.

The sooner you start on shorthand the better. Teeline is probably the system most used by journalists. The beginning standard is 80 words per minute. Classes are also often available at colleges.

Broadcast journalists need to be comfortable with cassette recorders and editing suites. Many colleges run media production courses which include instruction in a range of audio and video skills.

If you have no technical skills and want to be a press photographer, an evening class (or membership of a photography club) should help. Few classes, however, are likely to specialise in press photography.

Multi-skilling

Anyone working in journalism is likely to work in more than one medium. Try any (or all) of the items listed under *Skills* above.

English

Learning from reading and listening to both good and bad journalism is a fairly painless way to sharpen up your English. Keith Waterhouse is probably the practising journalist with the highest reputation for clear, concise English. He praised Wynford Hicks' *English for Journalists* (1993). It is really a kind of pocket reference book to be consulted regularly. It includes a useful guide to further reading.

Roger Fowler, *Language in the News: Discourse and Ideology in the Press* (1991) is given away by its sub-title. A critical linguistic approach to the uses to which English is put by journalists.

Although old and possibly difficult to find, Leslie Sellers' *Simple Subs Book* and *Doing it in Style* (both 1968) have been on the desks of a generation of newspaper journalists.

Get a good dictionary (Cassells is good on modern and technical English), and *The Oxford Dictionary for Writers and Editors*.

The media

The best general introduction to the media in Britain is Colin Seymour-Ure's *The British Press and Broadcasting since 1945* (1991), although it has dated quickly.

James Curran and Jean Seaton, *Power Without Responsibility* (1991 edition) is the standard undergraduate text. It covers a longer time-span than Seymour-Ure's book.

Ralph Negrine, *Politics and the Mass Media in Britain* (2nd edition, 1994) is also useful.

Michael Leapman, *Treacherous Estate: The Press After Fleet Street* (1992) is by a practising journalist.

Granville Williams, *Britain's Media – How They Are Related* (1994) is available from the Campaign for Press and Broadcasting Freedom.

Brian McNair, *News and Journalism in the UK* (1994) is the most current survey, and considers many of the changes facing journalism in the 1990s.

Roger Wallis and Stanley Baran, *The Known World of Broadcast News* (1990) looks at the effects of new technology on news and broadcasters.

Peter M. Lewis and Jerry Booth, *The Invisible Medium: Public, Com-*

mercial and Community Radio (1989) covers the issues in radio up to the end of the 1980s.

Peter Chippindale and Chris Horrie, *Stick it up Your Punter! The Rise and Fall of 'The Sun'* (1990) is a good introduction to the tabloids.

Bob Franklin and David Murphy, *What News?* (1990) looks critically at the provincial press.

Media 'revolution'

As well as keeping up to date, it is useful to learn something about the systems which have been superceded. Most journalists still remember hot metal.

Linda Melvern's *The End of the Street* (1986) is the standard work on the Wapping 'revolution'.

Suellen M. Littleton, *The Wapping Dispute* (1993) is both more comprehensive and deeper in its analysis. Neither is the last word on the matter.

Objectivity

Objectivity is addressed in McNair (see page 168). The Lichtenberg article is in James Curran and Michael Gurevitch (eds), *Mass Media and Society* (London, 1991), Chapter 11.

Ethics

The regulatory bodies mentioned in Chapter 12 all publish their adjudications and codes.

Ray Snoddy, *The Good, the Bad and the Unacceptable* (1993) is an important survey by the journalist who did most to put ethics back on the journalism agenda.

Andrew Belsey and Ruth Chadwick (eds), *Ethical Issues in Journalism and the Media* (1992) is much more academic. Otherwise there is little of UK origin. Most American texts are only tangentially relevant. Carl Hausman, *The Decision-making Process in Journalism* (1990) presents some interesting case studies and the reactions of journalists.

Getting started

The numbers of journalism manuals are multiplying almost weekly. None is particularly recommended. Rummage through them all.

UK Press Gazette, Campaign, Broadcast, PR Week, Media Week, The Bookseller keep you in touch with current developments and issues in the media, and with some of the jobs available. Get as much work experience as possible.

Starting salaries

Journalism makes very few people rich, and none fabulously wealthy. Salaries have been falling since the late 1980s. They vary enormously. The following applied in the spring of 1994.

Weekly newspaper in the north west of England: £8,200
Evening paper on the south coast of England: £9,100
Book editor (London): £9–10,000
Magazine editorial assistant (London): £11,000
Assistant information officer: £12,200
Press office assistant: £12–14,000
TV production assistant: £6,100–£13,800
BBC trainee: £12–14,000
Reuters graduate trainee: £15,000
ITN news trainee: £17,000

INDEX

advertising 60, 65–6, 71, 74, 79, 89, 91, 96, 117–18
alternative media (*see also* magazines *and* newspapers) 105–6
Associated Newspapers 45, 58, 68, 76
Northcliffe 74

BBC (*see also* radio *and* television) 13, 17, 20, 21, 25, 37, 43, 43–5, 49, 57, 65, 67, Figure 7.1, 76, 77–9, 83, 89, 92, 97–8, 99, 103, 112, 116, 120, 139, 143
Beaverbrook, Lord 54, 89
bi-media working 42–52
Birt, John 77, 97–8, 99
British Journalism Review 9, 19, 78, 89, 120, 162
broadcasting (*see also* radio *and* television) 64, 102, 105, 151
Broadcasting Act (1900) 75, 120
Broadcasting Standards Council 120
broadsheet (*see also* quality press) 7

codes (in journalism) 111, 113, 120, Figs. 12.1–12.5
Community Radio Association 141
copy 159, Fig. 14.1
 -flow 3–6
current affairs 34, 98, 154–5

editor/editing 3–5, 7, 15
EMAP (*see also* magazine publishers) 74, 139
English, use of 33, 36, 162–3
ethics 9, 15, 35, 110–120
European Journalism Training Association 119
Evans, Harold 86, 91, 107–8, 158

fanzines 106
features 7, 24, 138–9, 159
Fleet Street 10, 25, 37, 54, 71, 106
free newspapers 59, 63, 71, 73
freelancing 26–7, 138, 151–2

Guardian Media Group 68, 74, 83

Harmsworth, Alfred (Lord Northcliffe) 12, 18, 54

Henley Centre 78, 96–7

Independent Television Commission 120

Jameson, Derek 17–18, 37
journalist
 as professional 9, 14, 109, 101–5, 149–50
 background of 16–18, 21, 25–7, 35–6, 40, 149–50, 163
 Black and Asian 38
 education of 17, 25–7, 138, 143
 image of 10, 12–13, 99–100
 nos of 1, 14–15, 20
 pay 15
 science and technology, and 39
 specialist 18–19, 24, 35, 45, 157
 standard of 12–13, 100, 101, 110–20
 status of 14, 15
 student 149–50
 women 37–8

Knight, Andrew 50, 87

magazine publishers 35, 39, 60, 80, 82, 117, 139
magazines 17, 22, 25, 27, 60–2, 63, 65, 80–2, Table 8.1, Table 8.2, 91, 106, 117, 138–9, 141, 142, 143, 150–1, 154, 159
Major, John 94, 116, 117
Maxwell, Robert 66, 82, 116
media studies 35, 139, 142
Mirror Group Newspapers 42, 99, 114
multi-skilling 41–52
Murdoch, Rupert 50, 53–4, 56, 65–6, 68, 75, 82, 83

National Council for the Training of Broadcast Journalists (NCTBJ) 21, 139
National Council for the Training of Journalists (NCTJ) 14, 21–2, 23, 28, 31, 33, 111, 138–48, 149, 153, 155, 156, 163
National Heritage select committee 77, 113
national press (*see also* newspapers) 53–9, 68–71, 78, Table 7.1, table 7.2, 95

National Union of Journalists (NUJ) 1, 29, 46, 96, 111–13, 118
  Code of Conduct 111, Fig. 12.1
  guidelines on reporting homosexuality Fig. 12.4
  statement on race reporting Fig. 12.3
national vocational qualifications (NVQs) 21, 35, 138–9, 142
'new' technology 14, 15, 32–3, 39, 42, 49–52, Fig. 5.2, 55, 57, 58, 63, 64–5, 69, 73–4, 82, 150
news 11, 24, 30–31, 39–40, 54, 64, 79, 85–100, 102, 104, 138–9, 156–9, 163
news agencies 25, 83, 90, 139, 154, 157
News International 50, 66, 71, 75, 76, 80
NewsCorp 83
news room 3–6, Fig. 1.1, 43–4, Fig. 5.1
news sense 2, 14, 16, 94–100
newspapers (*see also* national press *and* provincial press) 10–13, 15–18, 22, 24–7, 36–7, 42–4, 47–8, 51, 54–6, 58–60, 65–6, 68–9, 71–3, 78, 83, 85–98, 100, 102, 106, 108, 111–14, 118–20, 139, 141, 150–1, 154, 158–9
Newspapers in Education Scheme 151

Pearson 56, 62, 83
Periodicals Training Council 21, 139
photography 107–9, 138–9, 151–2
Press Complaints Commission (PCC) 113–4
  Code of Practice 117, Fig. 12.2
Press Council 111–3
producer 3–5, 24
Prosser, Alan 20, 97
provincial press (*see also* newspapers) 39–40, 47, 53–9, 63, 71–4, Table 7.3, 78, 88, 95–7, 99–100, 142, 155, 156–7
publishing 54, 62, 82–4, 139, 142

quality press (*see also* newspapers) 11–12, 91
  journalism in 10–13

radio 59–60, 65, 79, 93, 99, 106, 139, 141, 143, 155, 159
  BBC Radio 45, 69, 79, 143, 154
  independent local radio (ILR) 45, 57, 60, 79, 143, 154
  Independent Radio News (IRN) 83
  World Service 47, 119
Radio Authority 120
Reed-Elsevier (*see also* magazine publishers) 54, 76, 82
Reed Regional Newspapers 74
Reith, Lord 78, 103

reporter/reporting 3–5, 7, 24, 28, 138
Royal Commission on the Press
  1947–9 87–8, 141
  1974–7 57, 85, 88

Scott, C. P. 11, 101
Sellers, Leslie 91–2, 158–9, 163
Shah, Eddie 65
shorthand 32
Snoddy, Raymond 118
sub-editor/editing 3–5, 8, 24, 28

tabloid (*see also* newspapers) 8, 92–3
  press 11–12, 47, 68–9, 91, 99, 112
  journalism 10–13, 77–8, 84, 93–4, 95, 97, 97–8, 113, 119
television 59–60, 61, 64–5, 70, 73, 75–8, 80, 92–3, 94, 97–8, 99, 106, 139, 159
  BBC-TV 15, 24, 25, 45–6, 50, 53, 59, 94, 154
  Channel 4 17, 26, 48, 78, 154
  Channel 5 98
  independent television (ITV) 17, 22, 26, 45, 48, 54, 75–7, 78, 83, 97–8, 154
  ITN 20, 21, 22, 25, 26, 42, 46, 49, 50, Fig. 5:2, 76, 83, 95, 139
  News at Ten 76, 78, 154
  satellite television 2, 17, 22, 75, 78, 143
  World Service TV 45
  cable television 75
Thomson, Lord 54–5, 56, 58, 65, 68, 89
Thomson Regional Newspapers (TRN) 40, 42, 50, 73, 74, 96, 139
training (of journalists) (*see also* NCTJ, NCTBJ *and* PTC) 13, 20–2, 28–9, 35, 40, 86, 138–48, 156
  provincial press, and 22, 25, 28
  qualifications 34, 138–42
  schemes 20–21, 31, 35, 139–48

UK Press Gazette 40, 46, 87, 90, 97–8, 100, 106, 108, 118
United Newspapers 68
United Provincial Newspapers 58, 74
United States of America 10–12, 15, 45, 47, 51, 54, 76, 83, 94, 102, 116, 118, 119, 149, 156
university 13, 16, 17, 25, 26, 36, 48, 74, 96–7, 138–41, 142–8, 156
  journalism schools 21, 26, 48, 142–8, 155

Wapping 65, 71
Westminster Press 5, 42, 43, 56, 58, 74, 83, 91, 139
work experience 138, 150–2